PSYCHE

The visionary potential of unusual states of consciousness

First published by Thorntree Press in 2016 through Lightning Source

Revised and republished in 2023

ISBN 978-1-9538821-9-6

for Anne
with warmest wishes

2023

Dedicated to the One

Butterfly Dreaming

I do not know whether I was then a man dreaming I was a butterfly,
or whether I am now a butterfly dreaming I am a man.

Chuang Tzu [369-286 BC] - Chinese Sage.

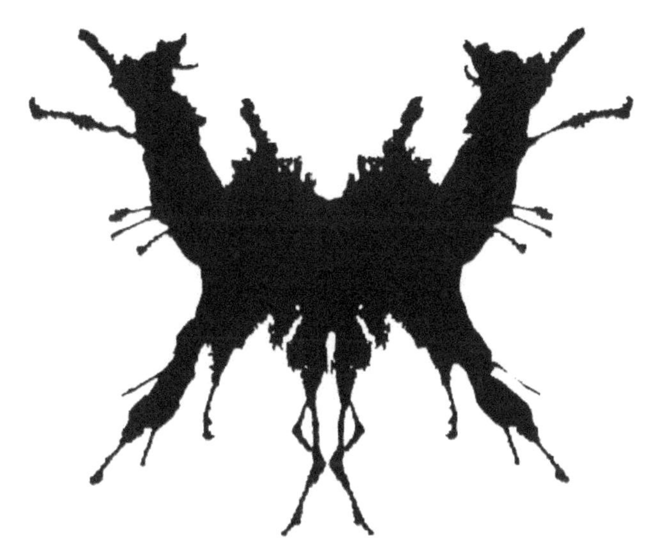

Contents

Introduction

PSYCHE is an exploration of the spiritual and creative potential of 'schizophrenia' and an exposé of state controlled treatments used to suppress people so labelled. It is an exposition that stems from first-hand experience. With visual and literal narrative, I present examples that highlight the visions and psychic insights that are prevalent.

Schizophrenia is commonly seen as delusional and hopelessly negative - this view is simplistic and woefully inadequate. Whilst acknowledging emotional turmoil, I emphasise such states can be channelled in ways which broaden the perspectives and perceptions of those affected.

It is not surprising that the subject of psychosis is fraught with misconceptions and misunderstandings. My objective however, is to provide clues that help the reader decipher the associated thought patterns in an endeavour to make this realm more intelligible.

I take the stance that *psyche-sensitivity* is an integral part of humanity's total mind, casting light not only on human nature, but also on the nature of reality.

We should accept and expect that our individual and collective evolution will involve intense struggle and unforeseen challenges. As the world around us becomes increasingly complex it is inevitable that our response to it, and life within it, also becomes increasingly complex. I see my experience in this context and as part of a continually developing process.

I encourage the reader to seek the many interconnections that dwell beneath and beyond the surface of these words and images, a matrix of concealed meaning will be revealed.

Please put aside your preconceptions and prepare to enter the inner reality of one diagnosed *psychotic*.

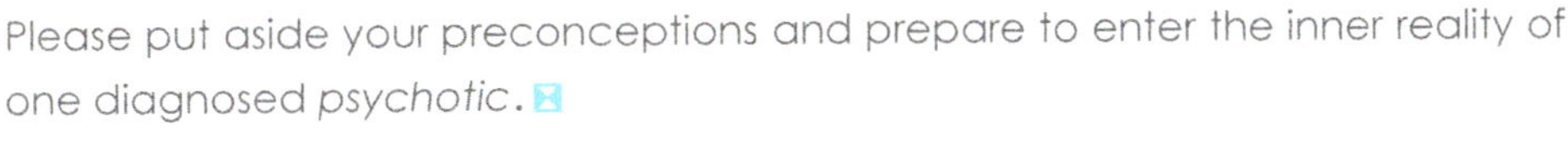 References to *schizophrenia* and *psychosis* are not meant to convey accord with current psychiatric orthodoxy; these terms are mentioned for expedience rather than agreement with clinical diagnosis. I use the expression *psyche-sensitivity* to counter prevailing assumptions and terminology.

Section 1: Magical Mystery Tour

We are part of a Universe of consciousness.
I sensed this out in space.
I devote my life to discovery of what this means for me
and for all humankind.

Edgar Mitchell - 20th Century Astronaut

Mind Reader

Extracted from:
The Oxford English Dictionary
and **The Oxford Companion to the Mind**

Psyche: The soul or spirit, breath, life, mind, love; represented as having butterfly wings. A butterfly.

Psychic: One who is particularly susceptible to psychic or spiritual influence.

Psychiatry: The medical treatment of diseases of the mind; hence psychiatrist.

Psychosis: The misapprehension and misinterpretation of the nature of reality.

The Butterfly Collector

Born into the world, a butterfly.

She takes to the air to experience the gift of life.

The collector [Prof: mg, od, ect, xyz, cert, psych, etc] interested in, fascinated by, ignorant of, the way of the butterfly, nets her and takes her from the natural environment back to his laboratory.

In captivity she is disorientated and fearful. She struggles to be free.

He observes her, recording the 'peculiarities of her behaviour' - important for his research.

He administers a measured chemical solution, hydrochloric acid.

Heavily sedated, she ceases to struggle.

He examines her *psychedelic* wings; 'intriguing'.

He inserts a sterilised needle through her thorax and pins her to a one-dimensional surface… her spirit breaks.

He attaches a label to her.

He is satisfied. She is categorised.

She is placed in a case and displayed behind glass.

He has his prize, another One to add to his collection.

How clever is he? What a curious specimen.

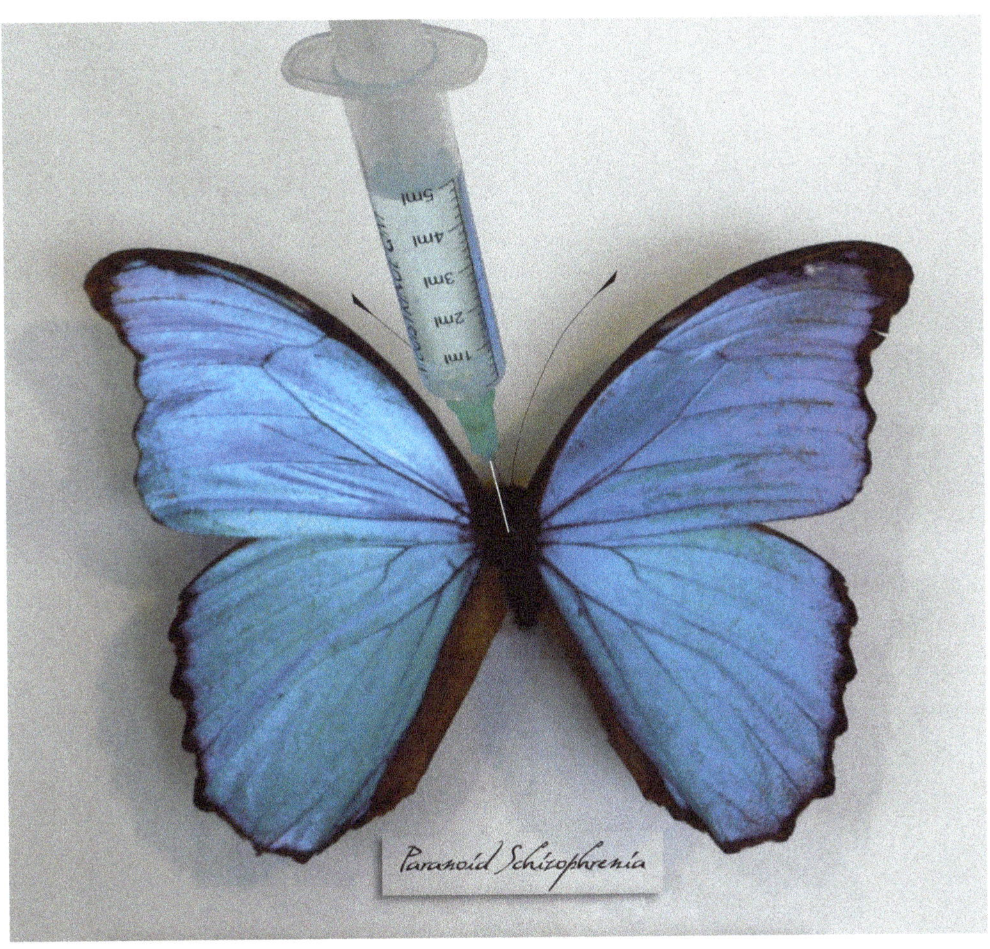
5ml
4ml
3ml
2ml
1ml
Paranoid Schizophrenia

Labelled

After leaving school at fifteen without qualifications, I entered the catering industry. In 1978 at the age of nineteen I worked as a chef at St George's Hospital, Tooting, South London. During my employment I experienced a sudden, dramatic shift in consciousness that changed the way in which I behold reality. I remember the circumstances vividly. I was sitting in the staff room reading a newspaper with my colleagues ...

> I stood up and announced: 'It's all wrong!'
> 'What's all wrong?' The head chef enquired.
> I responded: 'The world!'

Overcome with emotion, a flood of tears fell from my eyes. I left the hospital that morning after collecting my wage packet, leaving my career as a chef behind. I walked bare-footed to Balham where I rented a flat. On my way, I ceremonially withdrew £10 notes from my wage packet, released them one by one into the summer breeze, and watched them flutter through the streets of London like paper butterflies. Money had become completely irrelevant.

Arriving at my accommodation, I was instructed by an inner voice, to wrap myself in a white sheet and walk to Tooting Bec Common which was situated close by. ★

It was a glorious Indian summer afternoon, the scent of new mown hay hung in the air. On the Common, the voice told me to pluck a single acorn from an old oak tree. I did so, and after charging the acorn in my hand, placed it in my mouth and swallowed it whole. I had eaten from the *Tree of Knowledge*. This was the catalyst that created in me an exquisite sensitivity and psychic awareness.

★ *A-Z London Street Atlas: Edition 10, Grid Reference 3D-93.*

Having eaten from the *Tree of Knowledge*, on that same afternoon, I found the trunk of another oak that had been felled. I stood on the cross-section of this tree in my white shroud and outstretched my arms emulating crucifixion.

I entered a trance state, the sun caressed my face. I seemed to have access to a Cosmic secret. My trance state was broken by a man with an Irish accent who approached and addressed me with the words:

'You know something, don't you?'

'Yes I do.'

'Can you tell me what you know?'

'I know everything there is to know about not knowing.' I responded.

'Well then, can you tell me how to improve my golf?'

I must confess, I was of little assistance.

For a period after this, the most extraordinary and profound perceptions ensued. My relationship to time changed, days seemed like aeons; I experienced *The Eternal Now*.

Touch, taste, smell, sound and vision became acutely sensitised.

I realised *Christ Consciousness* and sensed a spherical energy field around my head. Stirred by a deep reverence for the sacred in creation, I felt as if I were at the centre of the Universe. I speculated, maybe every point in the Universe is also its centre. With an impassioned hand, I drew onto my bedroom wall, a large three-sided mantra/mandala:

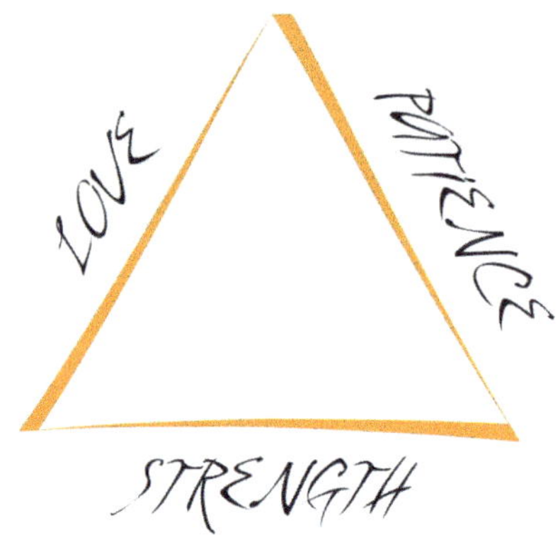

The voice persisted, increasing in frequency and clarity, communicating in a reassuring tone the words:

'Everything is going to be all right.'

My flatmates became perturbed by the sudden transformation from the person they once knew, to the new me, and the consequent changes in my behaviour [my actions had become ritualistic]. They contacted my family to take me from London back to Birmingham where I had lived in my formative years.

At home, family had legitimate concerns about the change in my persona, and eventually called for a GP who arrived with four additional clinicians. They interviewed me. I was affected by sleep deprivation; my dream world had encroached into daily life and my energy levels were excessively high. I requested an oral tranquiliser. Soon after I was pinned face down by all four clinicians and forcibly injected, needles inserted into each cheek of my buttocks - It felt akin to being crucified.

The syringe had discharged an excessively potent sedative. When I regained consciousness I found myself undressed in a bed on the ward of a psychiatric institution. My clothing had been confiscated.

I rose disorientated, walked naked through a corridor and approached a psychiatrist in an office who sat behind a desk. He informed me that I had been admitted as a 'voluntary patient'. I said:

'if I am a voluntary patient then I am volunteering out!'

I was told that before this could be permitted I would have to be 'assessed' by a panel of medics to determine if I should be retained for 'observation' and was promptly handed a pair of threadbare pyjamas; on reflection it is more than probable that my nakedness was recorded as a symptom.

Come the designated day and the appointed time, I entered a room with about ten seated clinicians forming a semi-circle armed with pens and note books, some pompously plumed with bow ties. I was placed in the centre facing them. This was evidently intended to be intimidating.

They proceeded to test my reality. I am aware of the crudity of these tests which do not take into account cultural differences, education, nuanced personal interpretation, the meaning of metaphor, or even a sense of humour. For example, it was put to me:

'What would you say to us, if we were to say to you,
people in glass houses shouldn't throw stones?'

'There's nothing wrong with throwing stones as long as you are careful.' I answered.

Immediately there was a frenzy of scribbling pens.

The *Thought Police* probed further:

> 'Why do you think you should be released?'
>
> 'Because I am strong.'
>
> 'We hope you are not too strong.'
>
> 'I am strong enough.'
>
> 'What will you do if we release you?'
>
> 'I shall join the Labour Party and fight the National Front.'

Again, pen was put to paper. It was at this point a diagnosis of *'Paranoid Schizophrenia'* was imposed upon me!

Some years later my mother shared the opinion of a respected family acquaintance, who during this time, was asked to determine my disposition.

> 'Elizabeth, you may well be the mother of the new messiah.'

Ma told me she buried her head in her hands and plaintively opined:

> 'Please God no.'

Thereafter, my mum, who was not religious, would send-up the likelihood of the second coming by quoting Monty Python's 'The Life of Brian':

> 'He's not the messiah, he's a naughty boy!'

Odyssey

I had become *One in a Hundred;* a teenage psychiatric patient diagnosed with schizophrenia.

I was told I must take *antipsychotic drugs* for the rest of my life. It is conceivable that had I accepted this literally I may not have experienced further shifts in consciousness. It is also conceivable, that had this been the case I would not have integrated my experiences and come to a subsequent understanding and resolution; consequently my life would have been impoverished.

There was a subtle and systematic attempt to condition me so that I would view myself as ill, diseased, and as experiencing delusional and hallucinatory states - 'cancer of the mind.'

During one assessment session I underwent, I recall a clinician stating:

'You are sick… do you know that?'

On replying: 'No I am not' I was informed that my answer clearly indicated I was and that until I had accepted this I would remain unwell. By saying I was not sick I was deemed to be insane, had I said the opposite the outcome would have inevitably and inescapably been the same… Catch 22.

Sadly, I began to see myself as deranged, until in 1984, I made the decision to extricate myself from psychiatric interference. I felt my identity had been sabotaged by diagnosis and fought to reclaim ownership of selfhood.

I have been prescribed antipsychotic drugs at various times and at varying levels, low and high. They have both helped and hindered, depending on the type of drug, efficacy, side effects and my personal circumstances.

I've experienced fifteen periods of schizophrenia spanning forty-five years. I seize every occurrence and do not regard them as disparate or isolated, rather as way-markers representing psychic events that have assisted me navigate this Earthly and Universal adventure. I have however, received psychiatric hospitality, mercifully, only five times ... 'Quoth the Raven!' As a *University of Life*, I have learned a great deal in intuitional settings.

The first and following episodes were pervaded by signs, symbolism, synchronicity and significance. As a result, in an endeavour to translate the transformational potential that psychosis possesses, having left the heat of the kitchen, I took up meditation [transcenmental medication] and decided to study art, with the aim of communicating my experiences using the language and vocabulary of visual media. I'm not eager to describe myself as an artist, preferring instead the more relevant and specific term *Reality Tester*. As a vehicle to communicate the experience of *psyche-sensitivity*, visual imagery is well suited; reality, illusion, metaphor and perception, a synthesis of the elements required to convey the complexities of the mind.

For many years I toured my work, and to earn a living became a Sign Maker ... I am not a normal schizophrenic, I am a professional schizophrenic!

It was not until I had rejected psychiatry that I was able to set into context and make true sense of my experience of unusual states of consciousness. I feel I've accessed aspects of reality few are privileged to glimpse, like an intrepid explorer who has journeyed to distant and mysterious lands and who has returned to present evidence of his discoveries.

Although I do not regard my experience as an illness, I acknowledge that during periods of schizophrenia assistance was required, but the harrowing ill-treatment I received at the hands of psychiatry intensified mistrust and neglected needs.

I am committed to the cause of exposing *Psychiatric Assault*. I do not fear schizophrenia - I do however fear its consequence, psychiatric intervention. Paradoxically it is the threat of intervention that persuades me to keep taking the tablets and live in prescribed reality.

I thank my lucky stars for a loving, protective, accepting family. In addition, I have a GP whose sensitivity, intelligence and open mind are a godsend, and I am embraced by a network of supportive friends and colleagues.

Receiving the label schizophrenia was possibly fated, but if I must be called 'schizophrenic', grant that it is not something I 'have' or 'got', it is neither an appendage nor something I have contracted, it is something I am. I regard my experience as a natural, integral and vital part of my personal evolution - a blessing, not a curse.

Insanity or Enlightenment?

R.D. Laing, an unorthodox psychiatrist, emphasised the link between the mystic and the schizophrenic; he stated:

> 'The mystic and the schizophrenic find themselves in the same ocean,
> but whereas the mystic swims, the schizophrenic drowns.'

I concur wholeheartedly, but point out that the so called schizophrenic can learn to swim ... given the opportunity. Often however, the schizophrenic is dragged under by the very people sent in to help.

Unlike the monks who prepare rigorously and systematically to attain and receive enlightenment, those who experience schizophrenia [the *psyche-sensitives*], I believe, have enlightenment thrust upon them, but in the absence of a disciplined spiritual foundation this imposed enlightenment is enormously difficult to cope with.

R.D. Laing also observed that insanity is:

> 'A perfectly rational adjustment to an insane world'.

The oceans of planet Earth are filled with a zillion salt water tears ... the sea of humanity. The trauma we experience as *psyche-sensitives* is often simply a painfully acute empathic response to the ills of the world. There is a fine line between fear for the world and fear of the world, and when this line is erased paranoia naturally ensues.

I am certain that schizophrenia is an expansion of our psychic capacity. I go further, I regard schizophrenia as not only a catalyst for personal transformation, but also for the transformation of our species; the evolutionary metamorphosis of humankind's collective consciousness. That may sound prophetic, but as a kindred spirit once remarked to me:

'Where would the Old Testament prophets be today
if they lived in our times and in our culture?'

The answer, which should not need to be spelt out, is in our psychiatric institutions. In other cultures, many who would undoubtedly be labelled schizophrenic had they lived in the West, are embraced by their communities as valued individuals who cast light on the dynamics of the Universe and our place within it; they are seen as chosen ones. The tide is however turning in the northern hemisphere and there is a *Spiritual Emergence Movement* in ascendance re-addressing such matters.

One of the many visionaries regarded by their contemporaries as 'outsiders' was the author Edgar Alan Poe, who would almost certainly have been diagnosed schizophrenic had such a label been available in the eighteen hundreds. The following vindication of Poe's genius was cited in *Schizophrenia, Creativity and Spirituality* - an obscure essay of the 1980s by Guy Stephens.

Edgar Alan Poe experienced an epiphany that unlocked deep cosmological insight, and in an inspirational outpouring he produced a work entitled *Eureka* which was published mid-way through the nineteenth century; coincidentally, the term *psychosis* was also coined then. At this time atoms were believed to be indivisible, irreducible balls of matter, the solid building blocks of the physical Universe. In *Eureka* it is revealed that matter is reducible to attraction and repulsion; some fifty years later physicists were to make the 'discovery' that confirms Poe's proclamation. He identified the Milky Way as an Island Galaxy before this had been established by astronomy. He stated that the Universe began as a single ball of matter that exploded, preceding the Big Bang Theory by seventy years, and also envisaged time and space to be one and the same, half a century before Einstein had even been conceived.

Edgar Alan Poe, his visions and his book, were dismissed as irrational, incomprehensible and nonsensical. One hundred and fifty years on, they are the unacknowledged cornerstones of contemporary scientific knowledge. An overt reminder of the falsely perceived superiority of scientific analytic experimentation over the validity of an individual's intuitive revelation.

I am not from a religious background, nor do I adhere to any one system of belief. I recognise all religions as possessing aspects of truth. Any religious body or individual that declares their way the only way, I regard as false prophets, or more accurately false profits.

I was an ardent atheist at nineteen, until via my illumination, saw and felt the expression of divinity in everything and everyone. I touched the Universal Mind, and know that God is not a reality ... God is reality, or to express this another way, Everything is, because God is Everything. I do not believe in God; I perceive God. In other words, I am aware of the consciousness of the Cosmos. The eyes of truth are watching. The archives of psychiatric institutions are well stocked with such testimonies, and why are these records retained? As evidence of insanity!

Saints, Sages, Seers, Shamans and Shivaists, through the ages, have been alive to the most extraordinary psychic experiences and often received transmissions in the form of voices; do psychiatrists regard them too as deluded? The limitations of accepted psychiatric norms make arriving at such a conclusion unavoidable. The other side of the coin however, is that by making such judgements and assumptions about others, psychiatry and its plaudits delude themselves. It is very convenient for society to classify a section of the community as 'the mad' for it produces the somewhat absurd notion that the rest of the population are normal.

The Oxford Companion to the Mind defines *psychosis* as:

'The misapprehension and misinterpretation of the nature of reality.'

Forgive my naiveté, but I was unaware that there was a correct way to apprehend and interpret reality; more to the point, I was unaware that there was consensus, let alone certainty, regarding the nature of reality at all. So, what is the nature of psychiatry's reality?

Written in the stars of the psychiatric Universe is the word, *Logic*. The law that governs their Universe was laid down in 300 BC by the Father of Logic, Aristotle:

'A must either be or not be A.'

To paraphrase, the world is flat. But as cosmologists and physicists look more deeply into the macro and the micro it is becoming very apparent that the Universe is a multiverse and the truth is reality is not logical and cannot be apprehended or interpreted logically, e.g. light is simultaneously a particle and a wave.

A can B, CDEFGHIJKLMNOPQRSTUVWXYZ [and not A].

The vision that is materialising before the very eyes of scientists is one that has long been seen by mystics. It is dawning that the mysterious Universe is also a miraculous Universe and the paranormal is the quantum, or multi-dimensional Universe in action.

It is not difficult to fathom why psychiatry has created the classification of psychosis, for if psychiatrists were to accept the validity of the testimonies of those who directly experience the multi-dimensional nature of reality, they would have to rescind the law that governs their Universe, which would in turn, invalidate their reality and by their own rules and definitions psychiatry itself would be certified psychotic! The stars would tumble and fall down from their sky and their ludicrous Flat Earth would be turned upside-down. So, psychiatry padlocks the doors of perception and pockets the keys and more false profits are made.

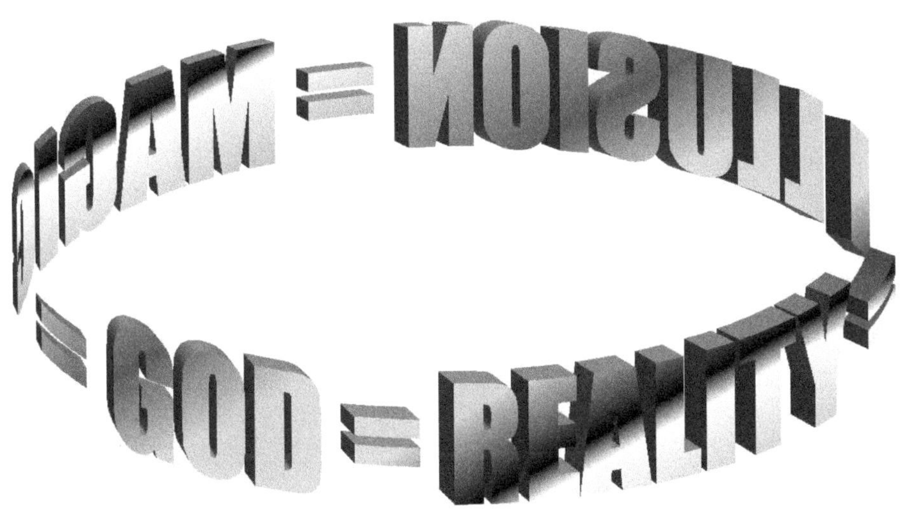

MAGIC = ILLUSION = REALITY? = GOD =

Godspell

When I talk of realising *Christ Consciousness,* I mean I experienced an awakened state, saw the world through new eyes, and felt the *Unity* that connects all things. With absolute certainty I knew my role within the Cosmic scheme. I imagined the sparkling stars as *Celestial Neurons* ablaze with intelligence, illuminating the *Universal Mind* ... the Mind of God.

It all made sense ... every particle, every atom, every molecule, every cell, radiates brilliance, converging and combining to form ingeniously innovative expressions of creativity: the tree, the butterfly, the human, the planet, the star, the Galaxy.

Stripping away layer upon layer of conditioned thinking, atheistic preconceptions and religious doctrines, I reasoned that if one defines God as Everything, then Everything becomes a confirmation of the reality of God. ☯

All that is within the Cosmos is inseparably bound up with the Cosmos. We are created and evolve from the stuff of the Cosmos, our physicality, our spirituality. We are conscious beings, and as such, our minds are manifestations of the Universe. Equally the Universe is a manifestation of our minds. In other words we are living proof that the Universe itself is conscious.

☯ The definition and description of God as Father/He/Him/Lord pertains more to the vested interests of male-dominated religious ideology than to the true nature of divinity. Whether or not we choose to use the word God to describe the consciousness of the Cosmos is unimportant, after all, God is not the word, God is a word.

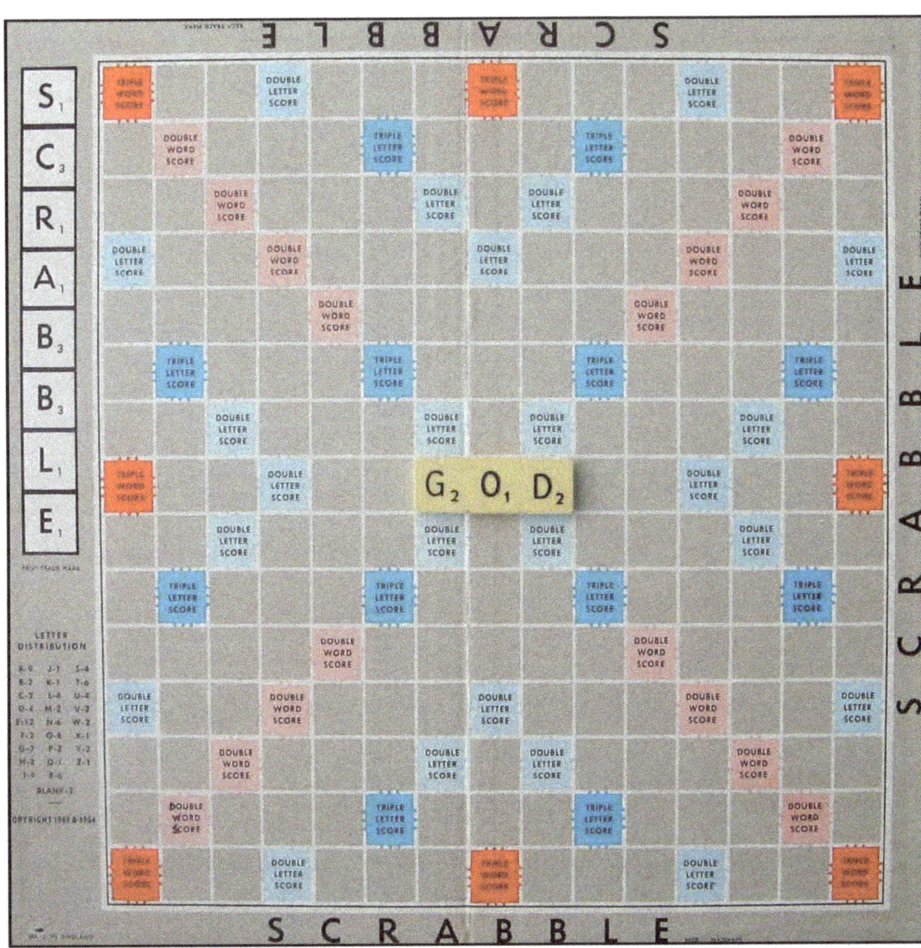

Beyond the Veil

If the Cosmos is conscious, it begs the question, for what purpose?

One night in bed, before turning out the light, I broadcast to God:

'Whatever you are, I love you.'

And then enquired:

'Why is there so much darkness in the world?'

During my sleep came a reply:

'I just shaded it in.'

We have a tendency in the so called 'developed world', to set ourselves apart from the natural world, by vainly declaring the inferiority of other life forms and fooling ourselves that we are in some way detached - us here, nature over there.

But whether we like it or not, we are as natural as the wind and the rain, the sun and the moon. You and I are no less, and no more meant to be, than anything or anyone else.

As such, who we are, what we are, our thoughts, our actions, are articulated through the prism of the natural Universe: kindness/cruelty - joy/sorrow - humility/arrogance - courage/cowardice - triumph/despair - dignity/shame - serenity/rage - love/hate - loyalty/betrayal - honesty/deceit - acceptance/denial - justice/injustice - dedication/indifference - wisdom/ignorance - sanity/madness - pleasure/pain - strength/weakness - optimism/pessimism - hope/fear ... all manifest by the Cosmos.

Could it be that we are a microcosm of the Universe? That the Universe too, must experience and assimilate a panacea of emotion in order to release and fulfil its potential, to feel, learn, become self-aware. Is life, with its myriad of possibilities and frightful extremities, vital to the Universe; enabling it to acquire deep insight, to grow, evolve? Maybe the expanding Universe is literally the expansion of the *Universal Mind*? God's consciousness, increasing and accelerating towards what? Big Bang? Infinite self-knowing? Eternal reawakening? Enlightenment? Rebirth? Genesis? ... God only knows!

For what it's worth, I sense that there is rhyme and reason, that we are not only part of a conscious Universe, but also a compassionate one; a Universe that seeks to understand itself through us, as we seek to understand ourselves through it, for beyond question, ultimately, its destiny is our destiny.

The Whole of the Moon

The reality of your nature is the nature of reality.

Your shadow is not present to act as your torturer, for it is the light that casts your shadow.

Your shadow is present to accentuate your light and animate your spirit.

The darkness of night sheds light upon the stars, and the stars shine so that we may navigate our soul's journey.

Truth lies within paradox. If there were no darkness there would be no illumination.

Light is God's shadow - Reality God's dream.

To be guided by light and darkness is the way to strike balance and actualise *Unity*.

Section 2: Visions

And those who were seen dancing
were thought to be insane
by those who could not hear the music.

Friedrich Nietzsche - 19th Century Philosopher

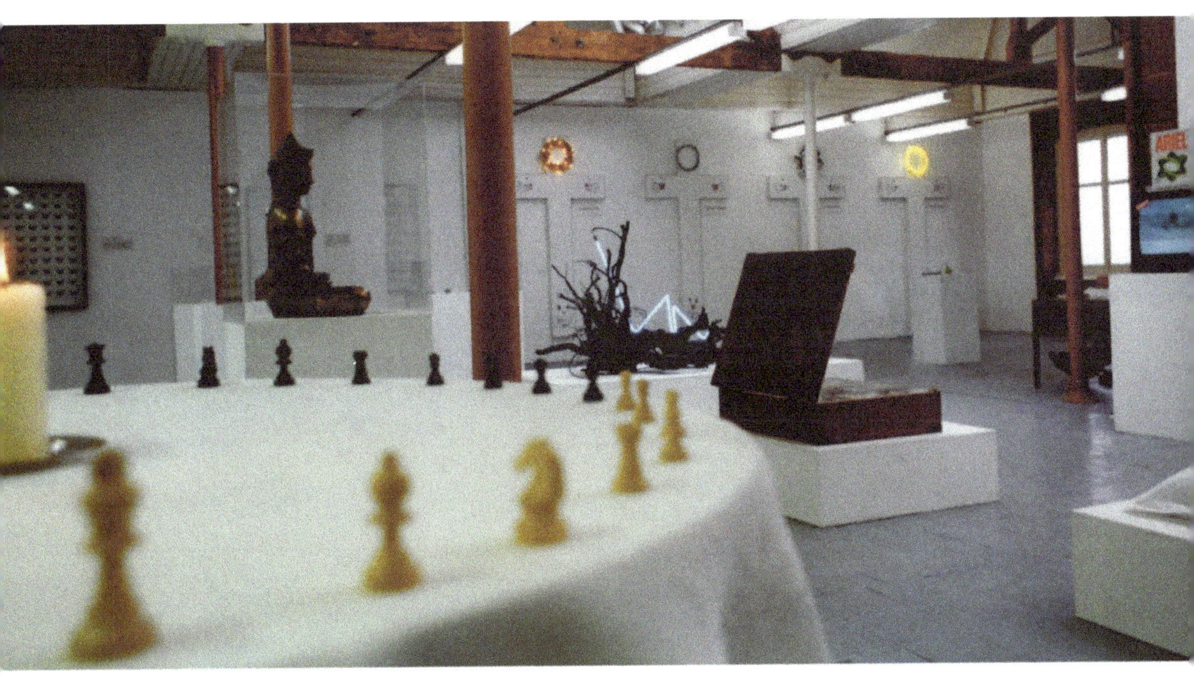

A. One in a Hundred

One person in every hundred is labelled *Schizophrenic*. The One is presented as a butterfly; the remaining ninety-nine, [not all together seriously] as *Rorschach's Psychological Inkblot Tests*.

Psyche is the Ancient Greek word for Butterfly.

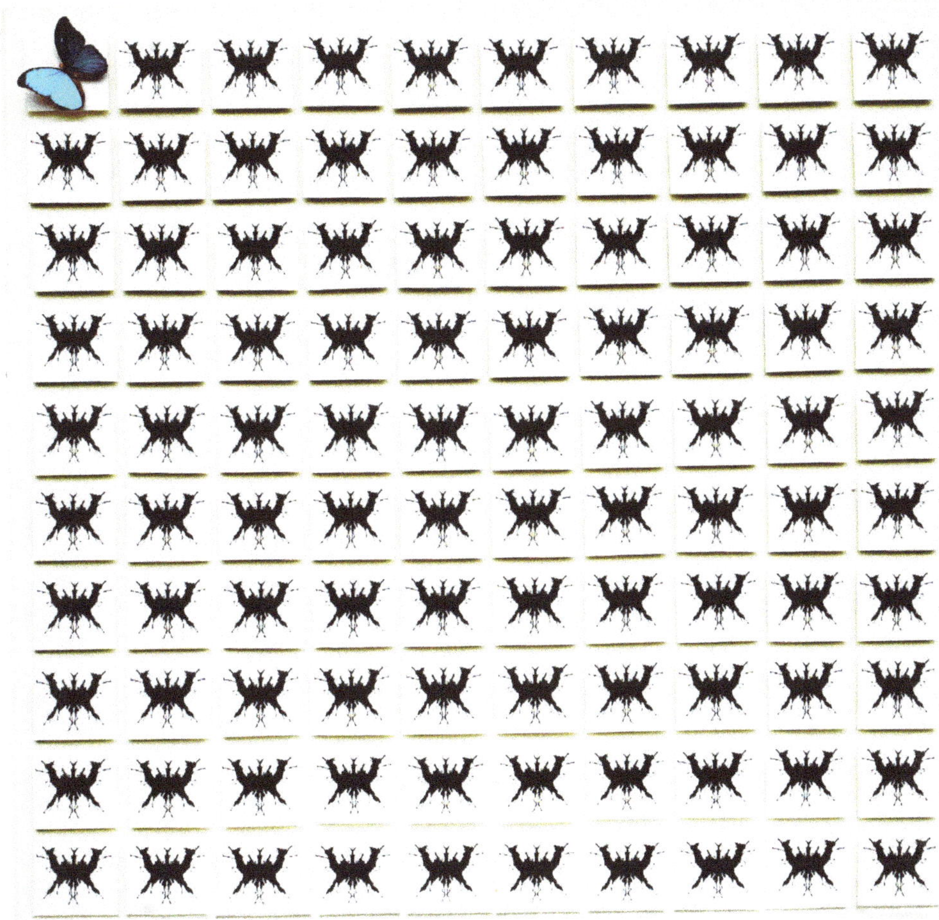

B. The King and I

I felt the spirit of Christ embodied within the statue had been transmitted to me. Immersed in bliss, I perceived the warmth and tension of a halo around my head. I believed I was Christ incarnate. It is difficult to convey the intensity of this mind-set except to say that it was overwhelming, confirmed by a voice within that said:

'You have been chosen.'

The statue became a shrine. The white feathers represented feathers from the wings of an Angel. The yellow dot or 'bindi' on the forehead united the holy figure to me as I also adorned myself with such a mark. The lines that polarise the figure I called a *Power Point.*

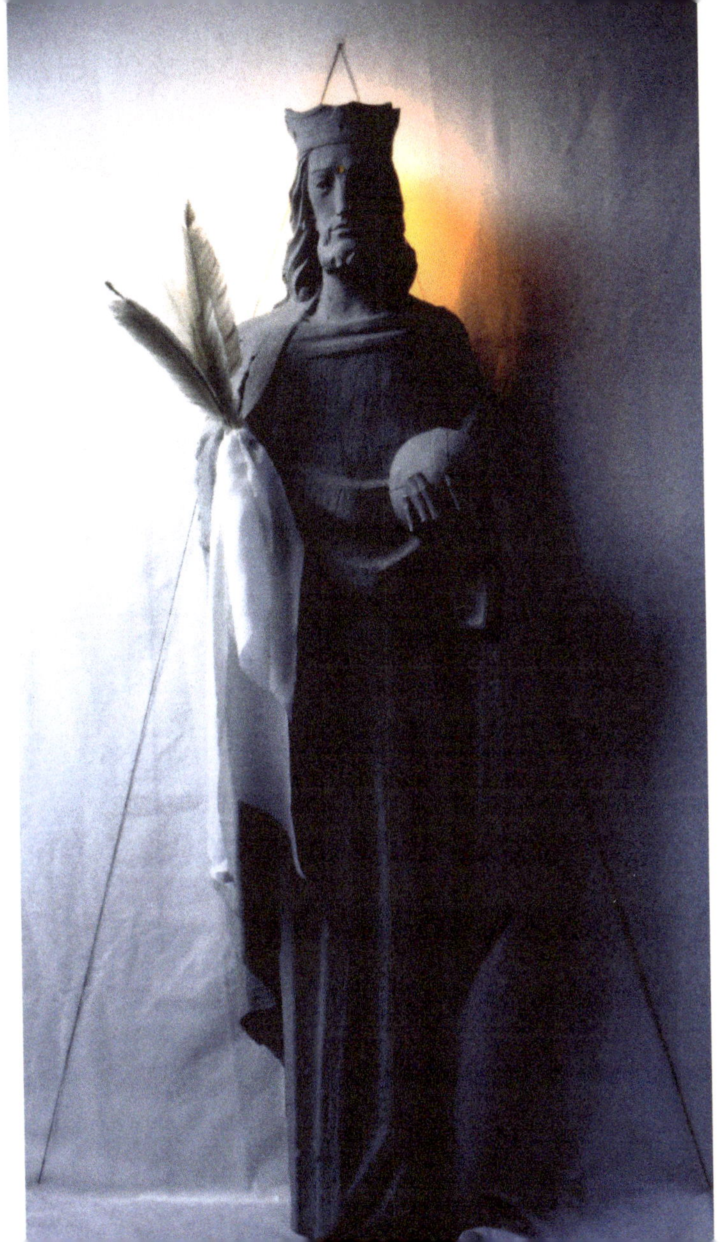

C. Masterpiece

His Masters Voice trademark took on significance, confirming that the voice I was hearing emanated from a higher authority.

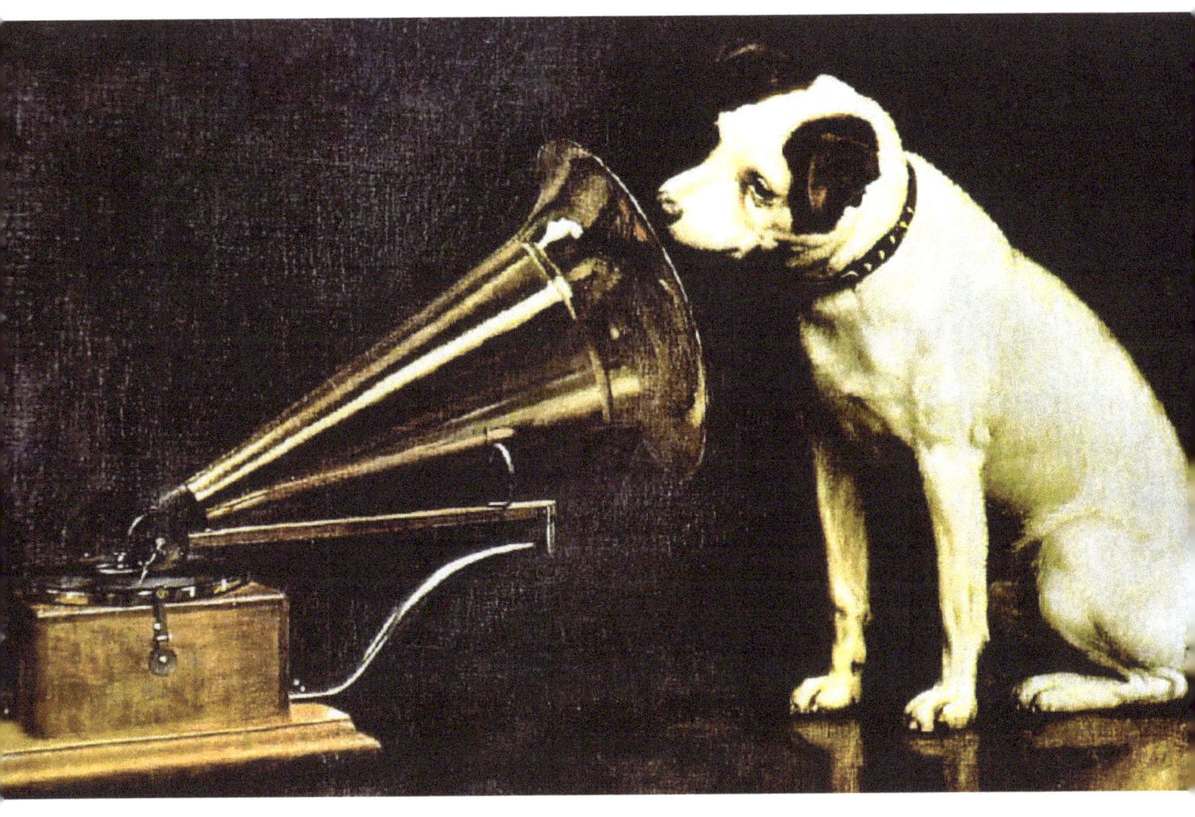

D. Thirst for Life

The plumb-line acted as a point through which Cosmic energy was passed into a vessel containing my urine. When I felt the liquid was sufficiently charged I drank it to receive the energy.

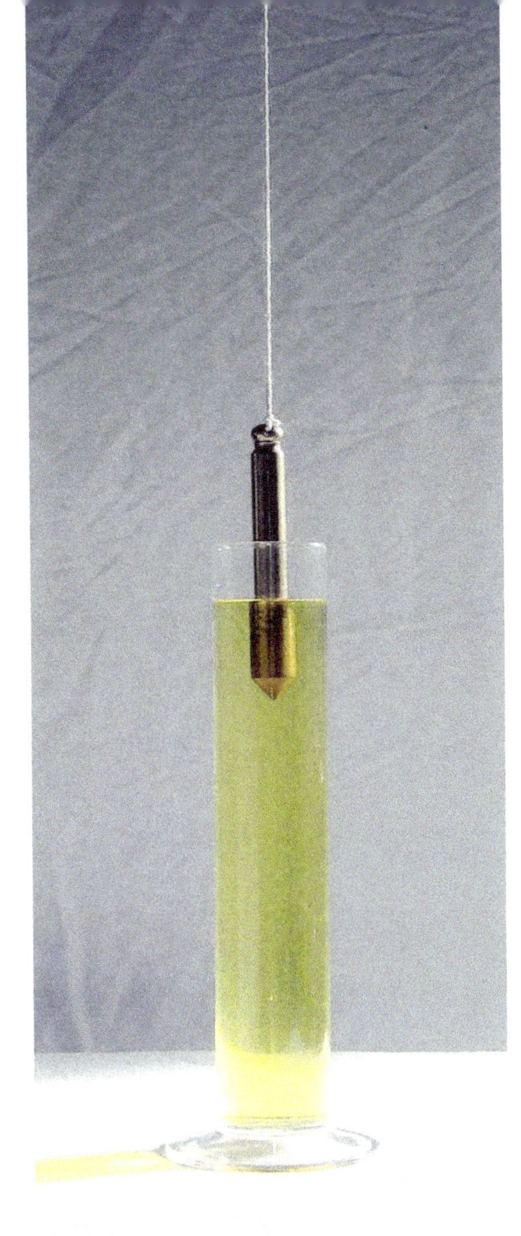

E. Head Case

At times I felt tremendous pressure and acute pain in my head to such a degree that I thought I was about to have a brain haemorrhage. In an effort to relieve the pain I projected the pressure through a G-clamp and into a pillow; soon after the pain and pressure subsided.

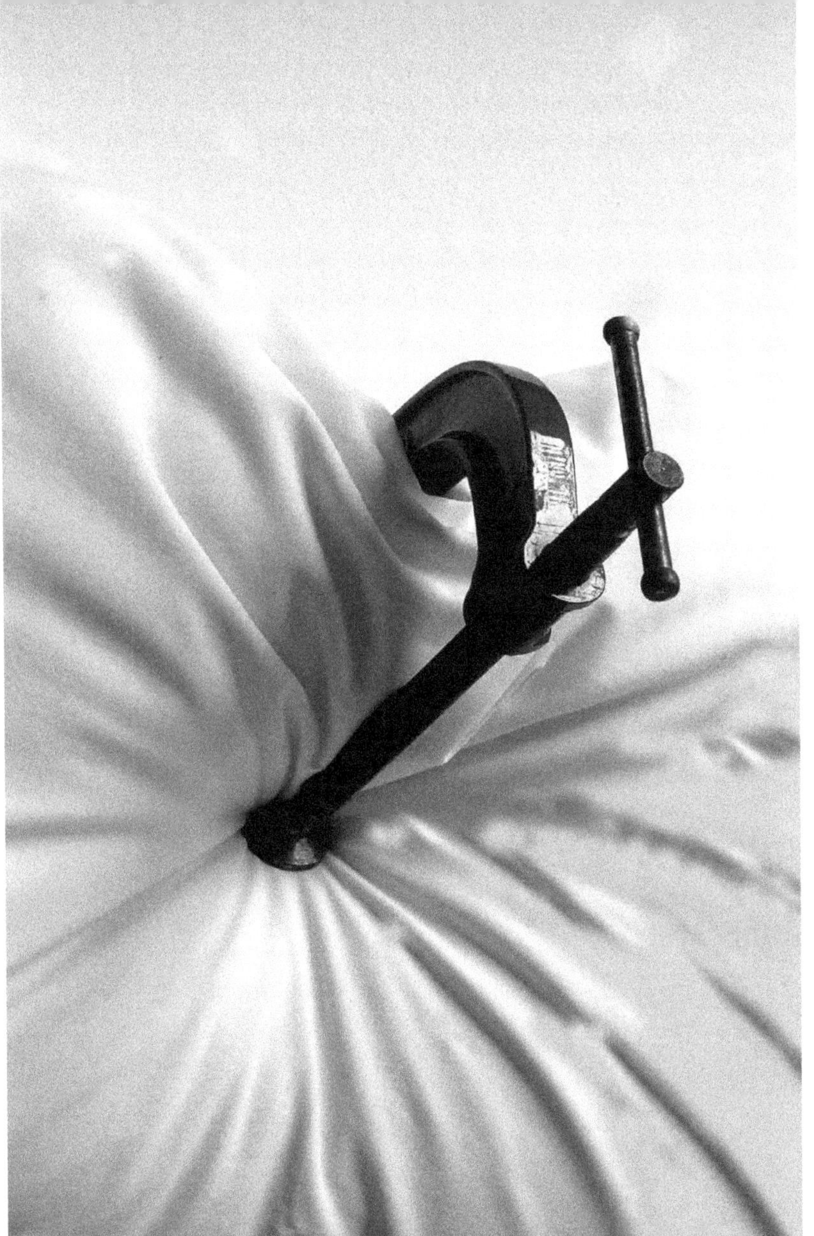

F. Hall of Mirrors

I felt that people were observing me from behind mirrors. In an attempt to deter them I would cover mirrors with toothpaste and carefully selected pages from books ...

I spy with my little eye someone beginning with 'P'.

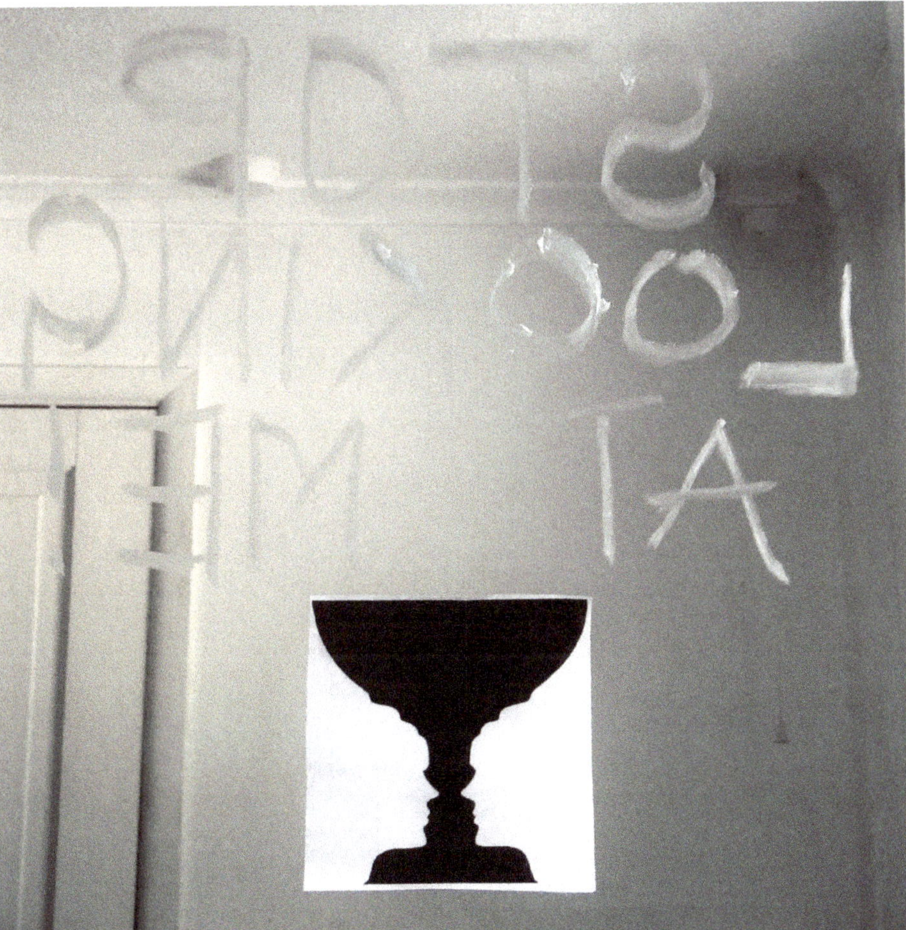

G. Battlefield

I sensed the forces of light and darkness in conflict on the streets of Birmingham where I was living at the time. These forces were represented with chess pieces.

I made moves with the pieces that were directly affected by the events occurring in the city. I would sometimes spend many hours through the day and night listening to the radio, taking instructions, and making complex manoeuvres involving calculations using geometric instruments. The moves were prompted by news broadcasts, weather reports, the chatter of presenters, phone-ins, lyrics and police transmissions.

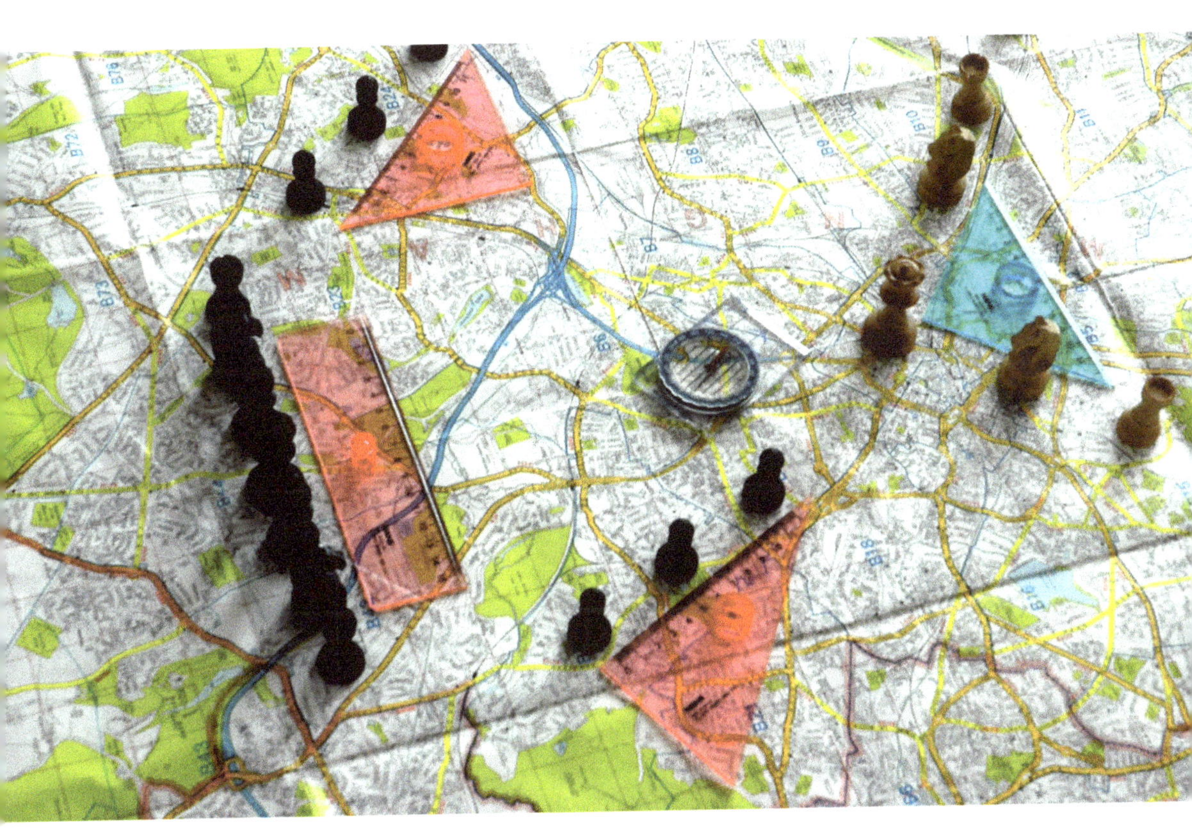

H. Lune

I believed that the moon was directly controlling my mind. The thinking that lay behind this belief was that the moon affects the oceans; human beings are composed of 70% water. Therefore my deduction was that the moon affects body and mind as powerfully as it influences the tides. During this phase I drank large quantities of H_2O.

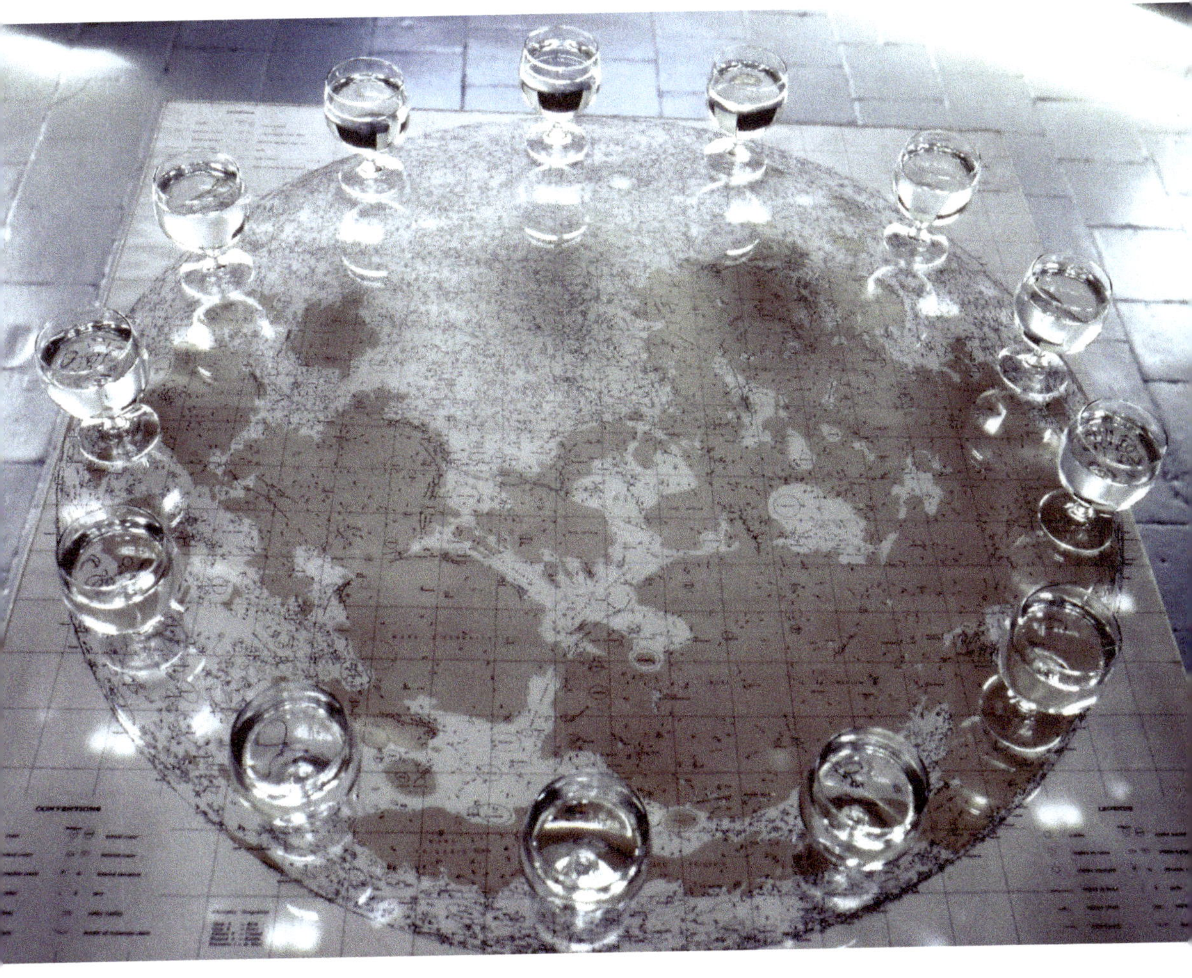

I. Food for Thought

I took the phrase 'you are what you eat' literally and ate various artifacts ranging from printed information through to magnets.

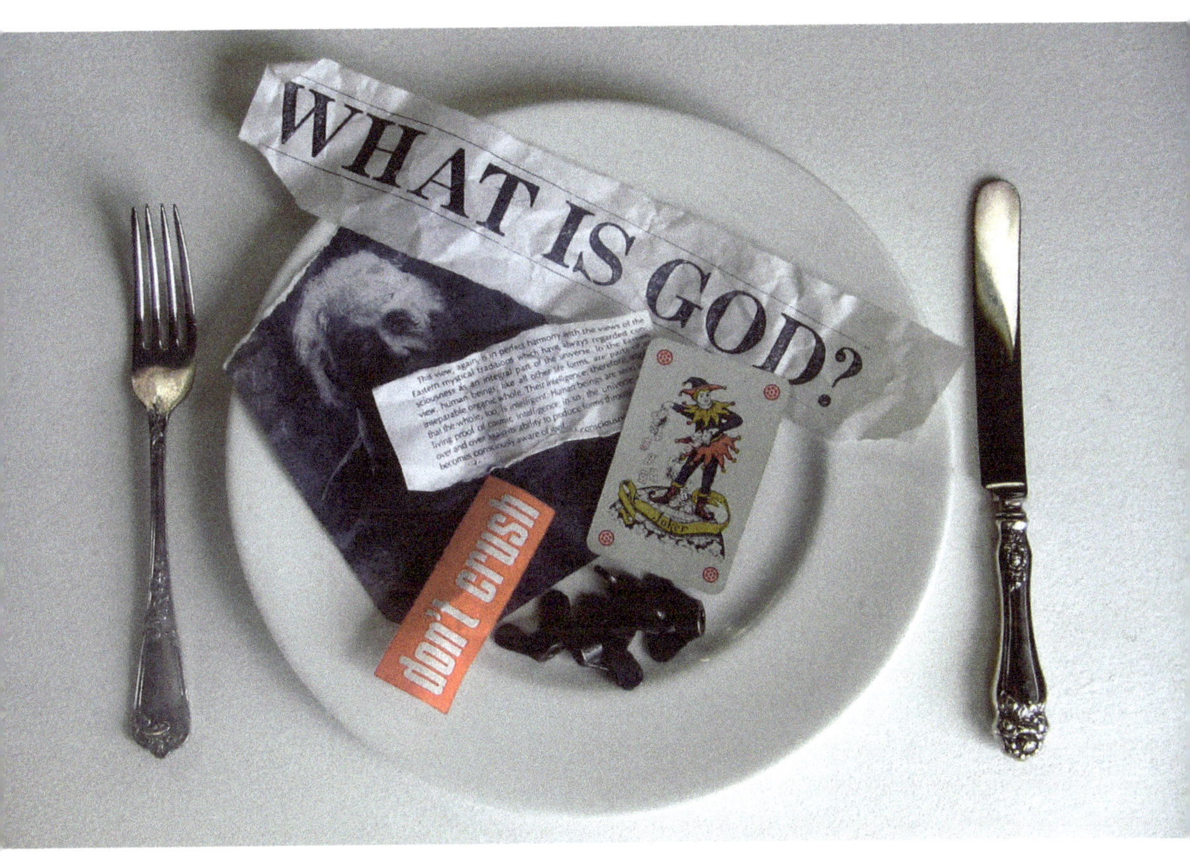

WHAT IS GOD?
don't crush
Joker
This view, again, is in perfect harmony with the views of the Eastern mystical traditions which have always regarded con- sciousness as an integral part of the universe. In the Eastern view, human beings, like all other life forms, are part of an inseparable organic whole. Their intelligence, therefore, implies that the whole, too, is intelligent. Human beings are seen as living proof of cosmic intelligence in us, the universe over and over again's ability to produce forms through which it becomes consciously aware of itself.

J. Mind Games

The black circle represented the Universe, the paper stars the Galaxies. The ball symbolised planet Earth and held a second significance - The games people play on personal and international levels.

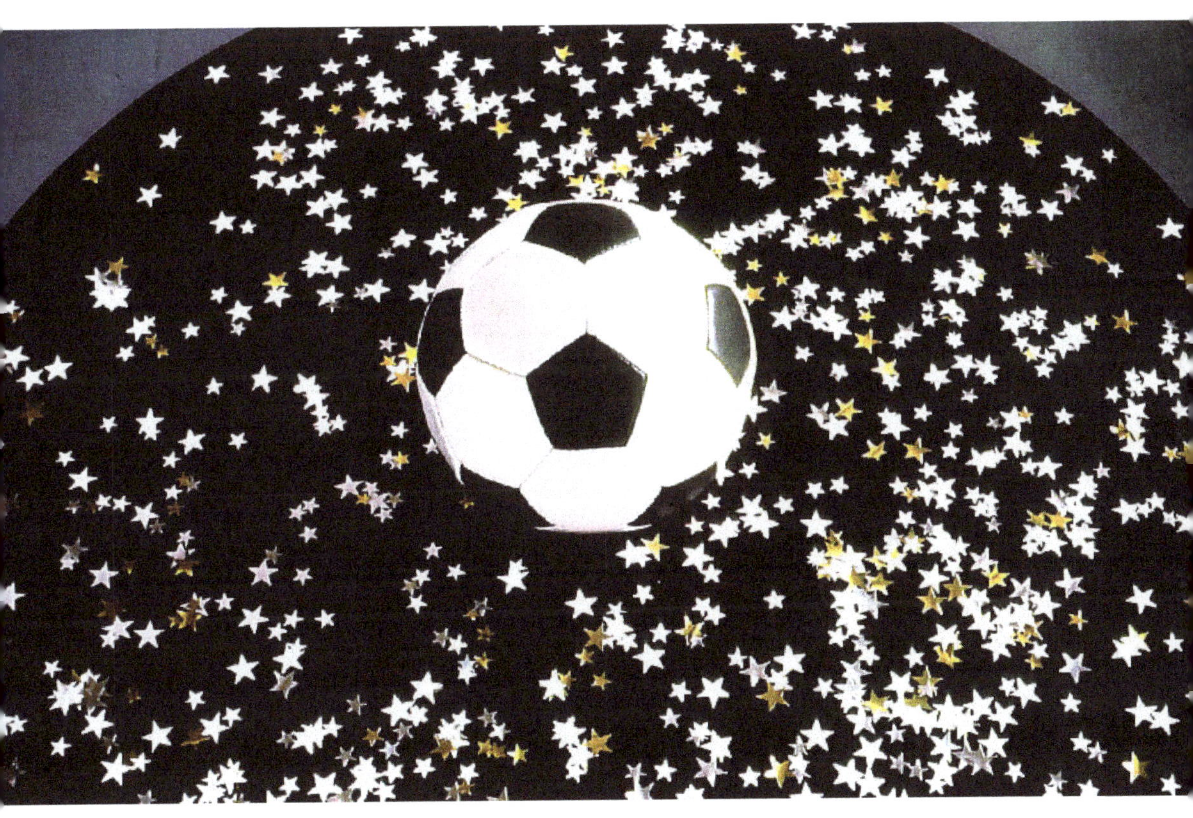

K. God does not Play Dice

Numbers assumed great importance. One of my compulsions was to throw dice on to a star chart and make numerical calculations that determined the position flint must occupy. In no way did I feel chance had any part to play in the falling of the dice, it was all pre-ordained.

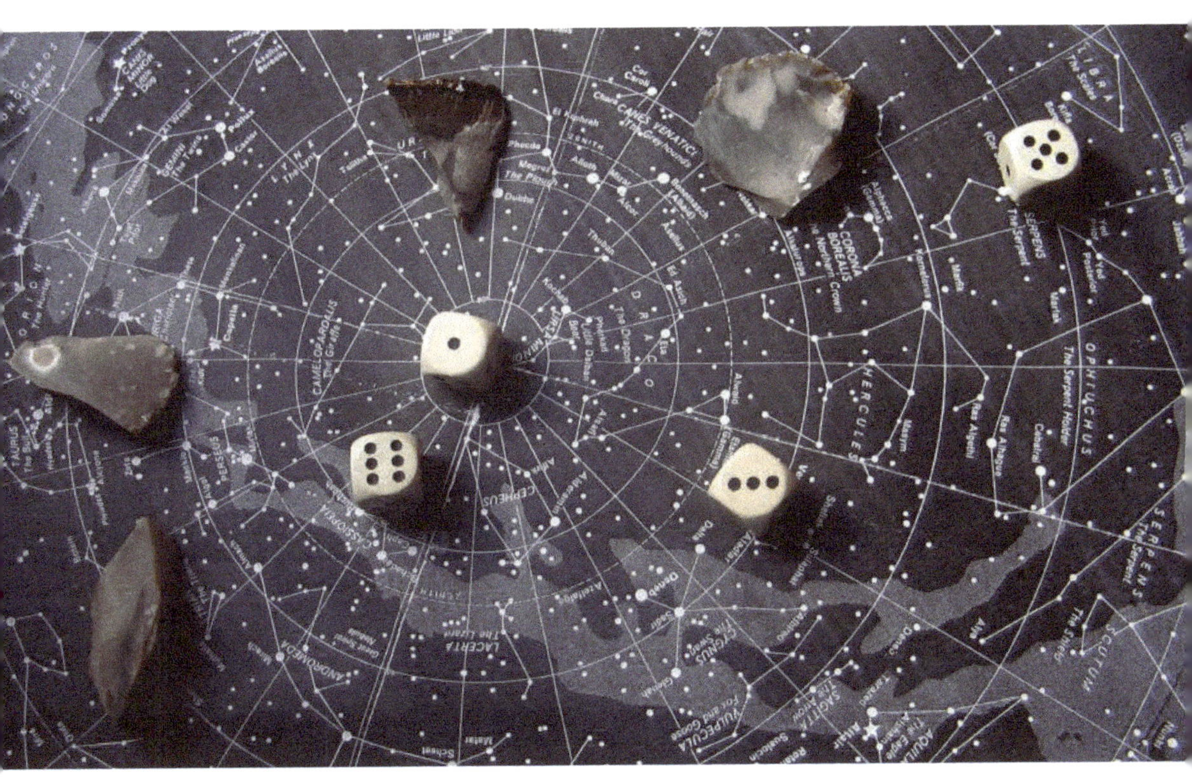

L. Remote Control

On placing a box of *Ariel Automatic* washing powder upon the television set not only could I see the people behind the screen, but felt they too could see me. I did not regard this as threatening. They would perform, converse, pray and applaud both to and for me. I would also take instructions and commands from the television and act upon them. The tasks I was told to undertake were sometimes of an urgent nature ...

'Buy now!... Pay later!'

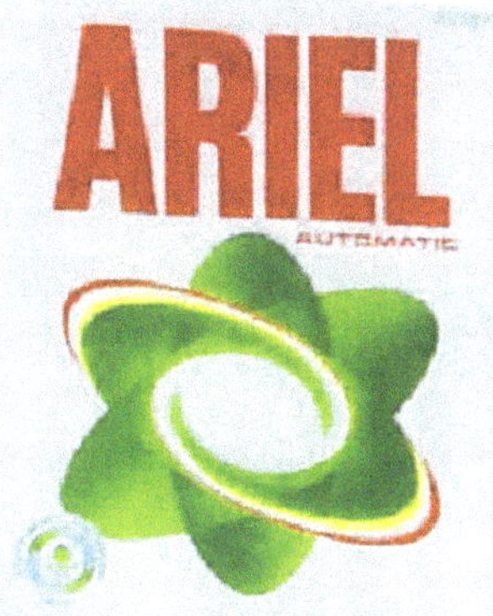
ARIEL
AUTOMATIC
cleans tough dirt, stains and odours
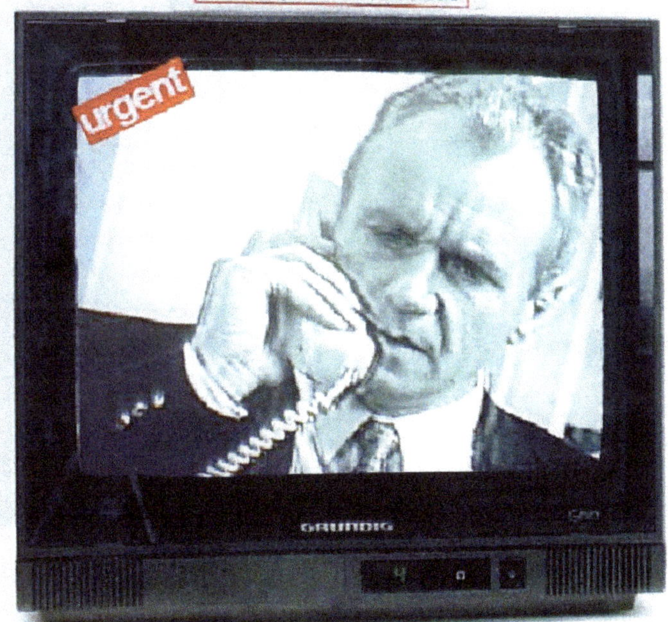
urgent
GRUNDIG

M. Life, the Universe and Everything

Einstein's equation of $E = mc^2$ seemed somehow incomplete, so I altered it with the addition of = OM, the Hindu mantra or chant meaning God. The addition of divinity provided an elegant solution to the mystery and meaning of the Universe... *God is relative.*

E+mc^2 =OM ®
108 01 42

N. Heal Thyself

I would paint with antiseptic and sometimes cover my body with the lotion. I felt that by applying the disinfectant it would heal and cleanse.

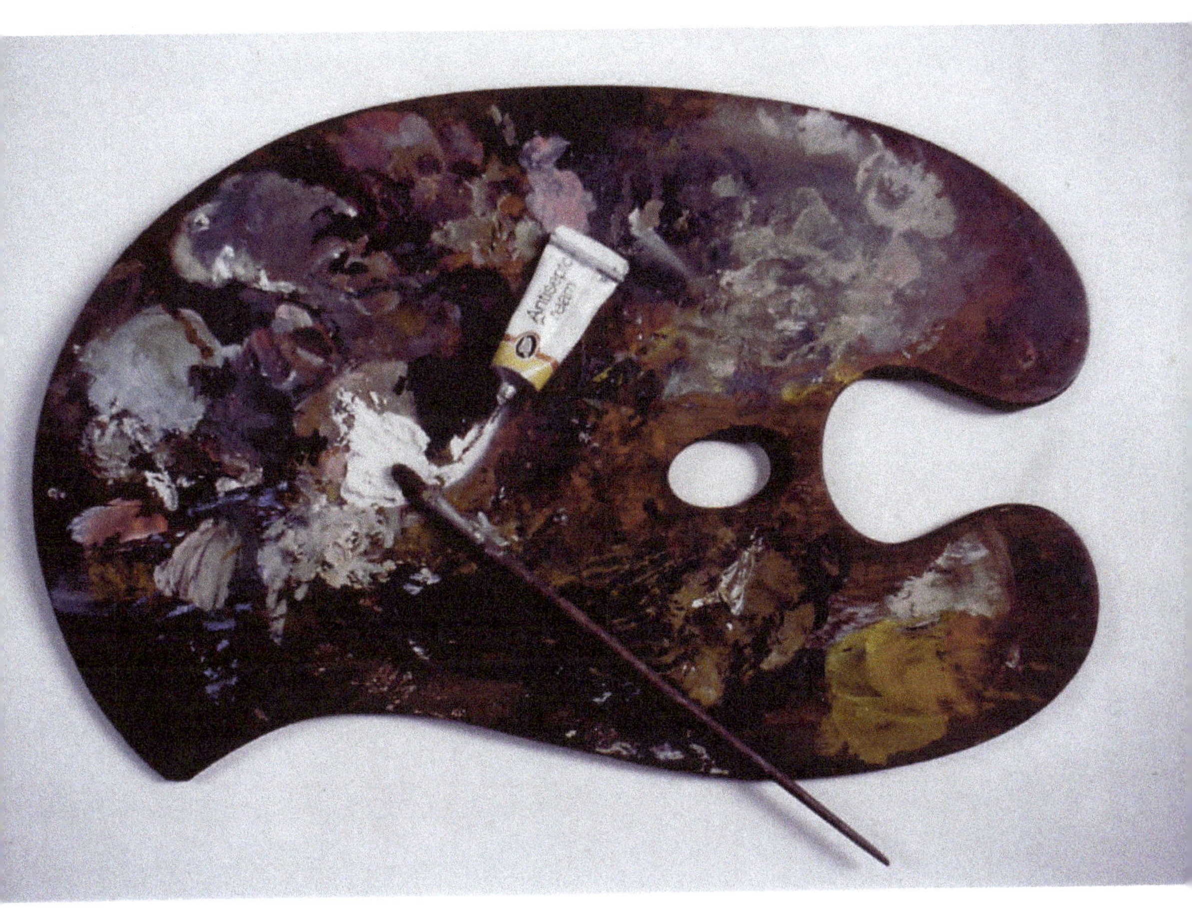

O. Disappearing Act

I believed that if I covered myself in a white veil I became invisible. This invoked the sense of being protected.

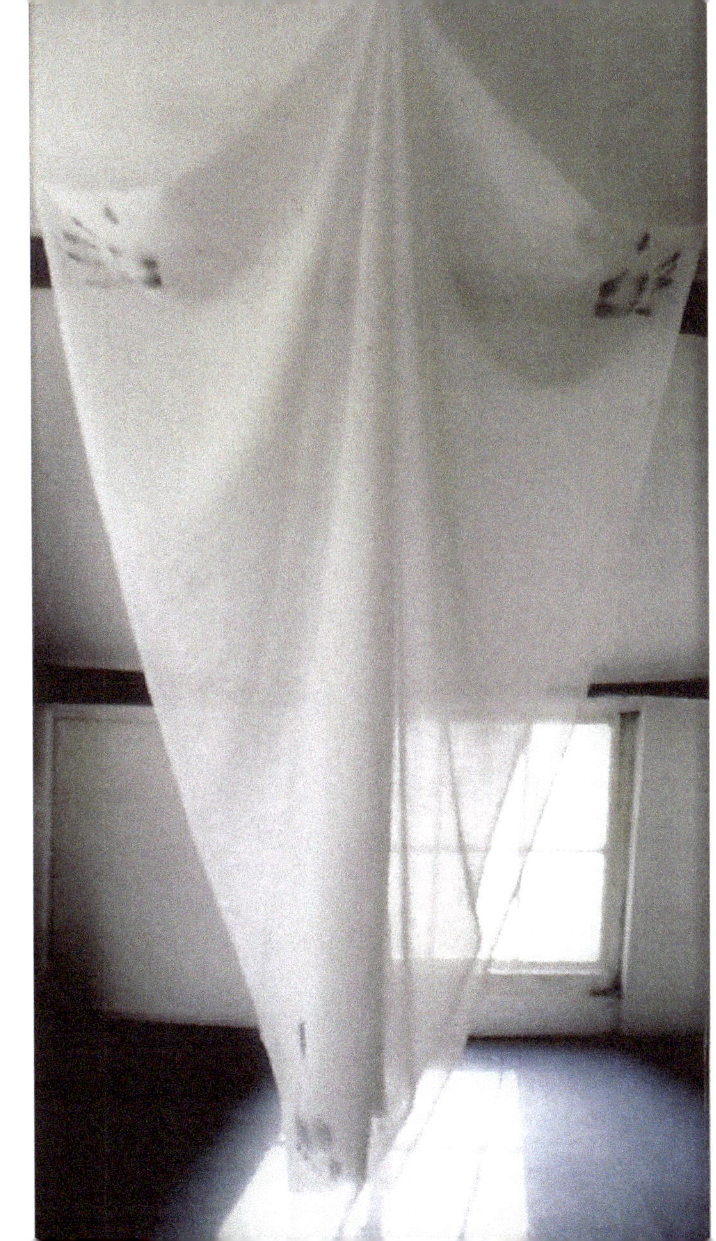

P. Written in the Stars

The *Milky Way* chocolate bars were inseparably bound up with the Galaxy itself. This exemplifies how the meaning of familiar things changed and took on Universal significance. Similarly wheels represented the *Wheel of Life*.

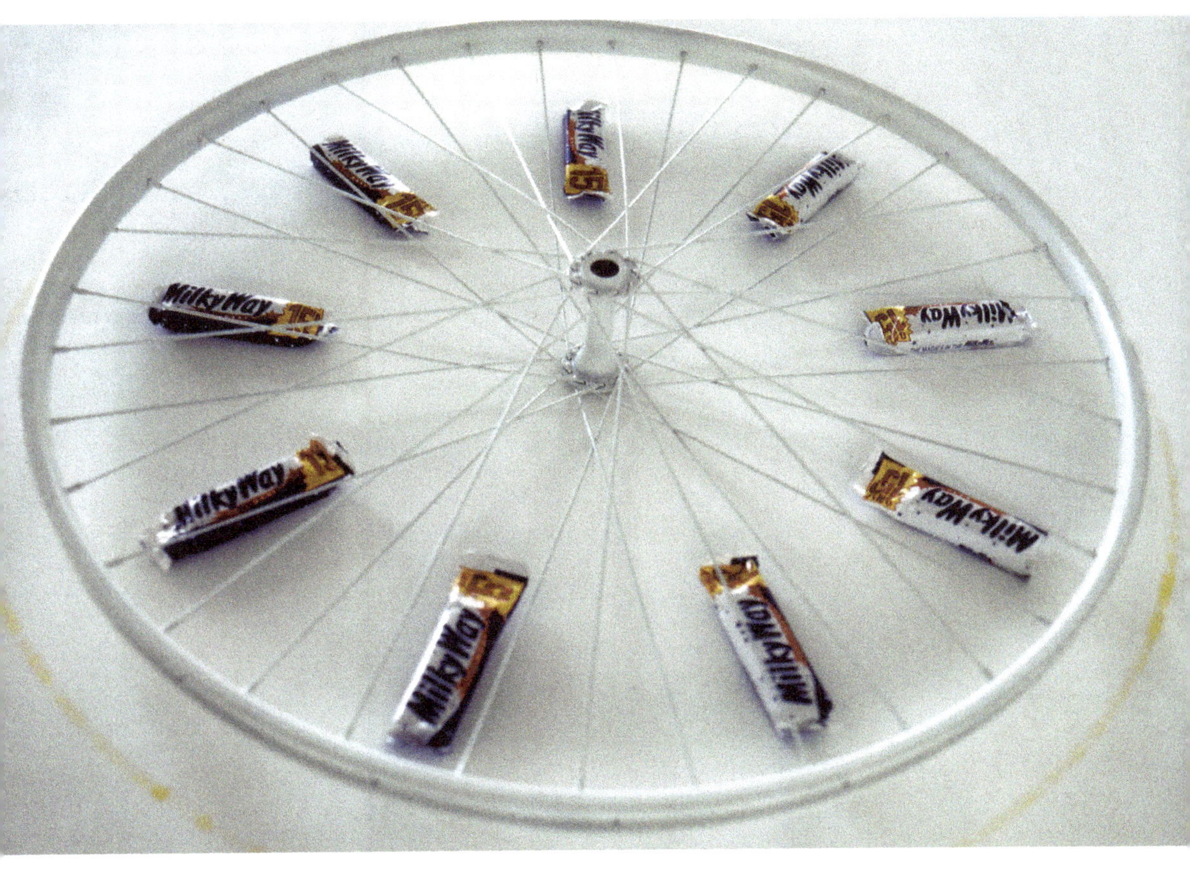

MilkyWay
MilkyWay
MilkyWay
MilkyWay
MilkyWay
MilkyWay
MilkyWay
MilkyWay

Q. Words of Wisdom

An interconnection was also felt with the toothbrush which literally represented the wisdom of its brand name.

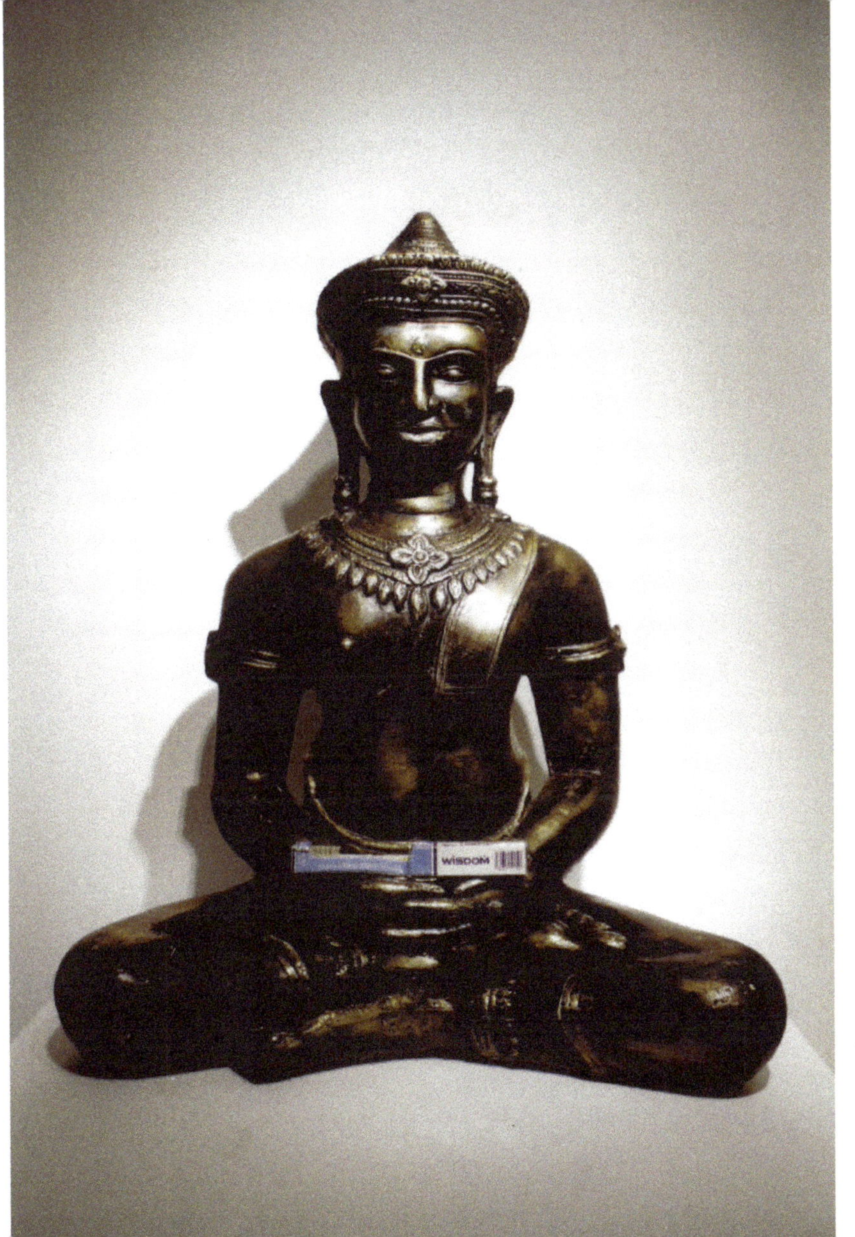
WISDOM

R. Electric Apple

I connected an apple via an electric cable to a tape recorder and attempted to listen to the sound it made. I heard *white noise*. This I took to be the voice of the apple.

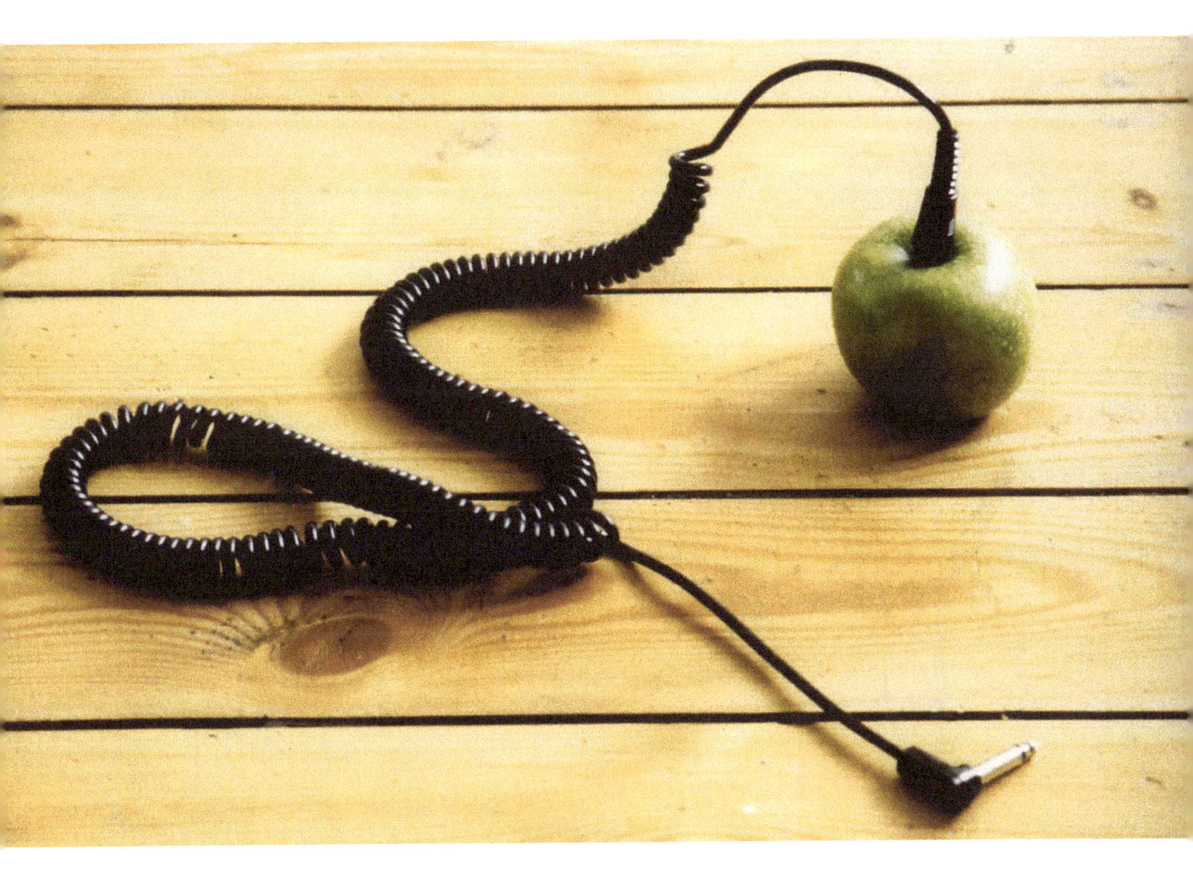

S. Sign

This was a road that was of great importance to me; a road for all Saints. I would make pilgrimages to it, a continuation of my spiritual preoccupation.

ALL SAINTS RD 14

T. Pie in the Sky

Another conviction was that beings from the heavens would come to take me from this planet. This I welcomed. I made plans in preparation for the event and kept a packed suitcase. Occasionally I would take the suitcase to fields where I would signal up into the night sky with a torch in an effort to hasten their arrival and my departure… I live in hope!

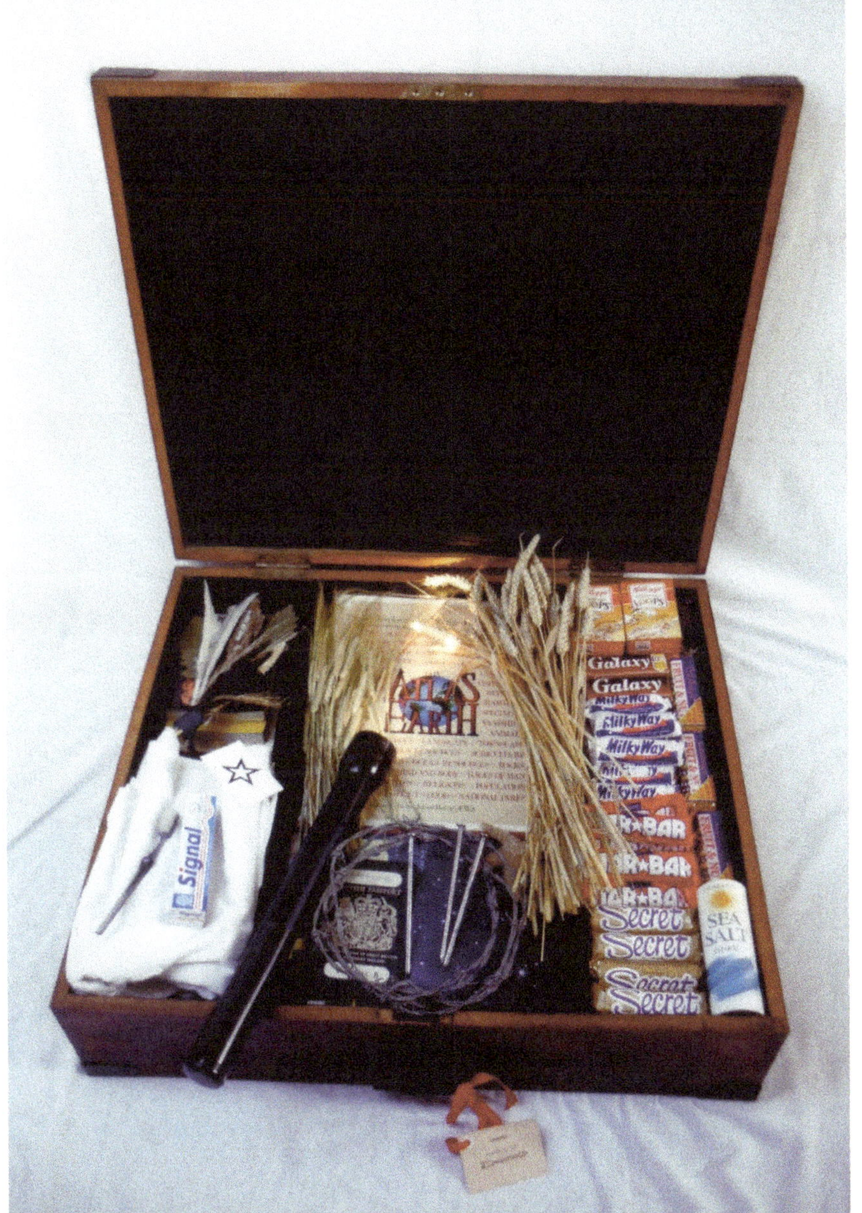

Signal
ATLAS EARTH
Galaxy
Galaxy
Milky Way
Milky Way
Milky Way
Milky Way
Milky Way
TRACKER BAR
TRACKER BAR
TRACKER BAR
Secret
Secret
Secret
Secret
SEA SALT

U. Transmitter

A *Power Point* was the name I gave to anything resembling a spire, from pylons to pine trees. *Power Points* would, I believed, receive and transmit the *Cosmic Pulse*.

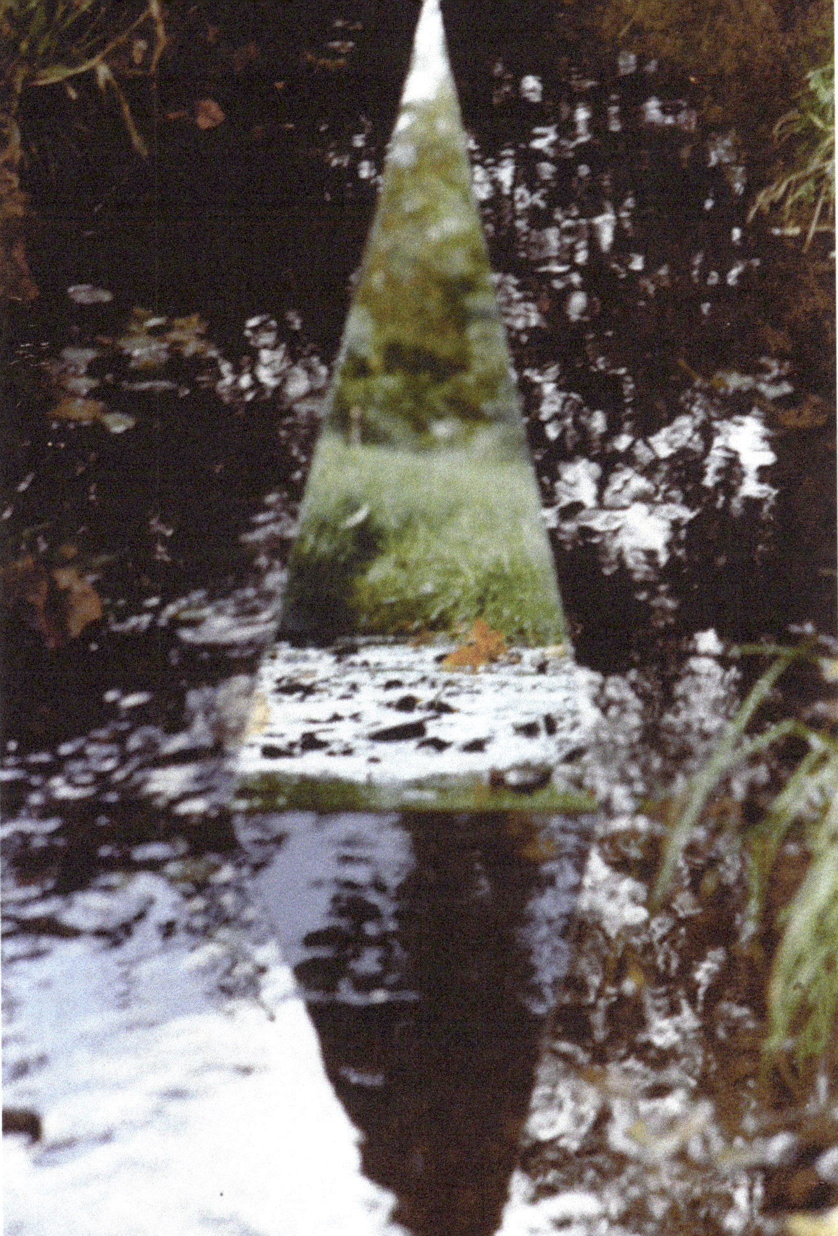

V. Unity

I removed chess pieces from the *Battlefield* and placed them in a circle to form balance. A lighted candle placed in the centre symbolised *Unity*. This formation echoes the Taoist Universal principle of *Yin and Yang*.

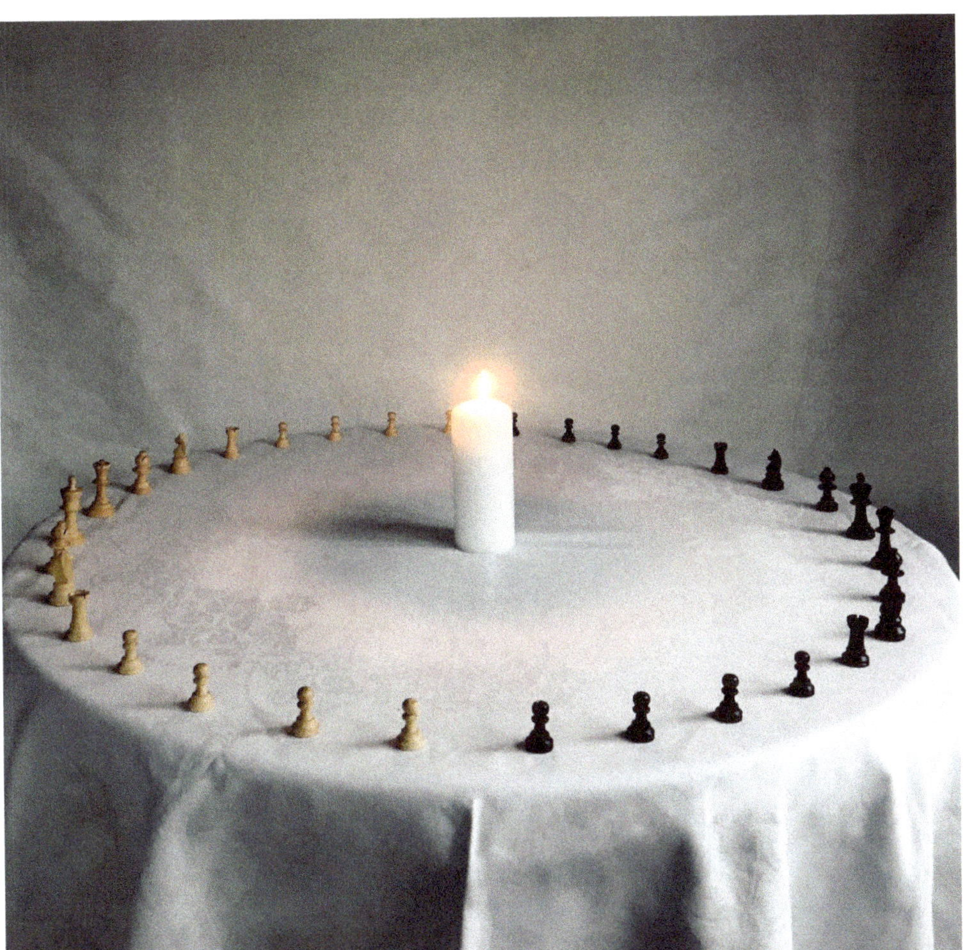

W. Brainstorm

Indicative of the power and energy that is felt during a schizophrenic event and conveying the way in which it can strike out of the blue.

The network of neurones that transmit and receive messages in the brain are tree-like and signal via electrical impulses.

It is said that ordinarily we use only one tenth of our brain capacity consciously. Schizophrenia feels like the unconscious 90% surging to the forefront of the mind and becoming fiercely alive.

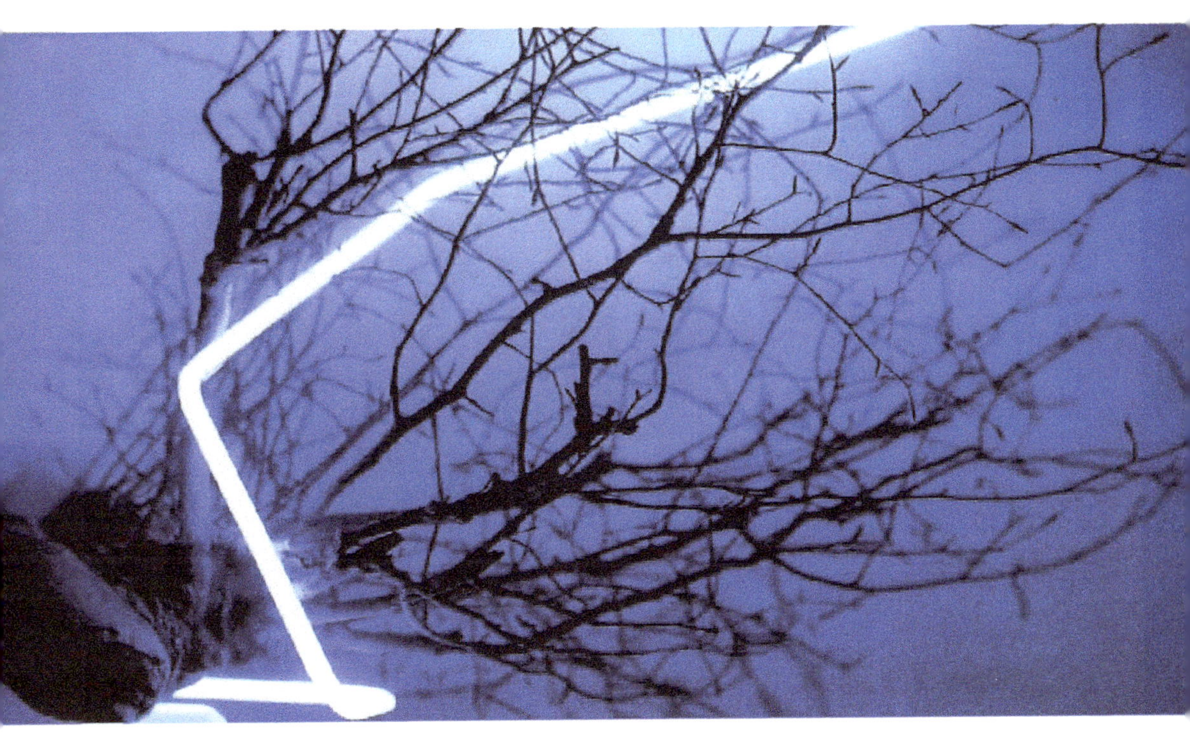

X. Method in Madness

Logic has been represented by the sequential numbers and letters around the perimeter of the grid. The break with conventional thought patterns has been illustrated by perforating the ordered structure.

Although *schizophrenic rationale* does away with commonplace logic, reason is integral to this state of being but is encrypted in metaphor.

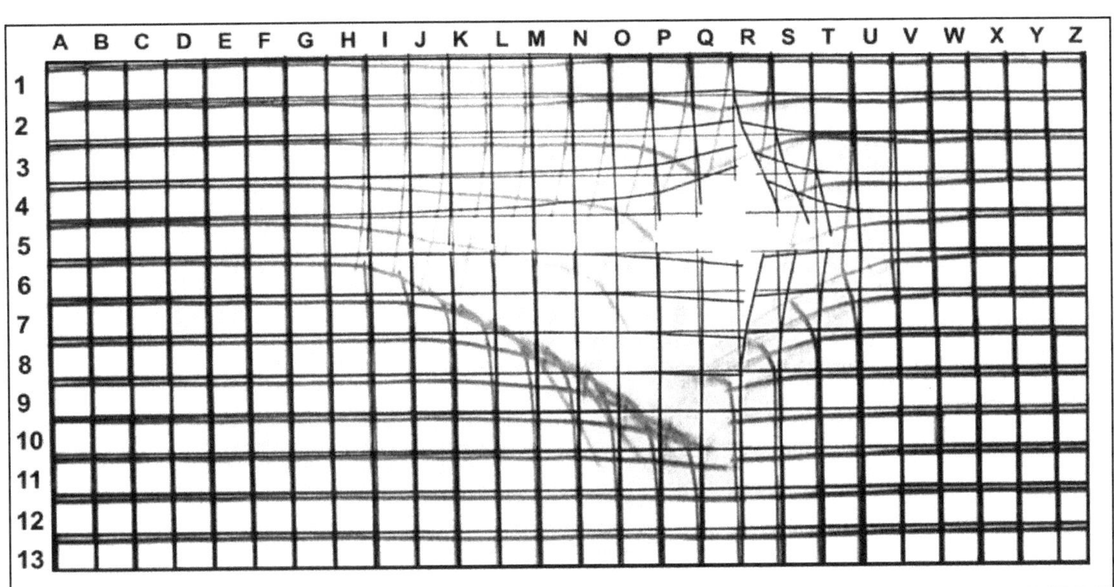

Y. Medication Time

I was told I must take *antipsychotic drugs* for the rest of my life.

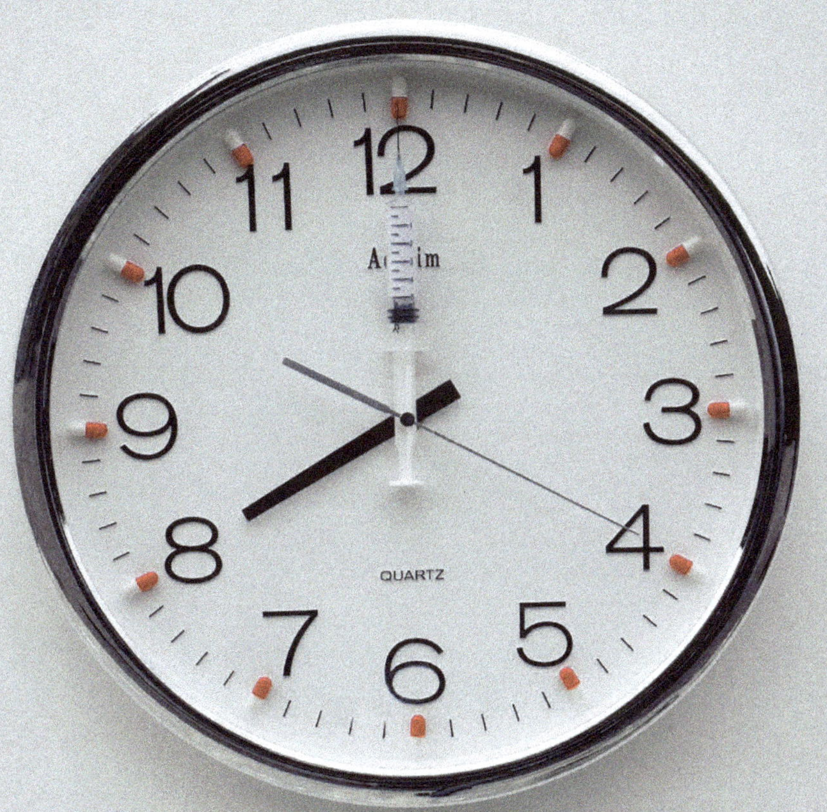

Acctim
12
11
1
10
2
9
3
8
4
7
5
6
QUARTZ

Z. Only Smarties Have the Answer

A reference not only to the drugs that are imposed on those who experience schizophrenia, but also to those who administer them.

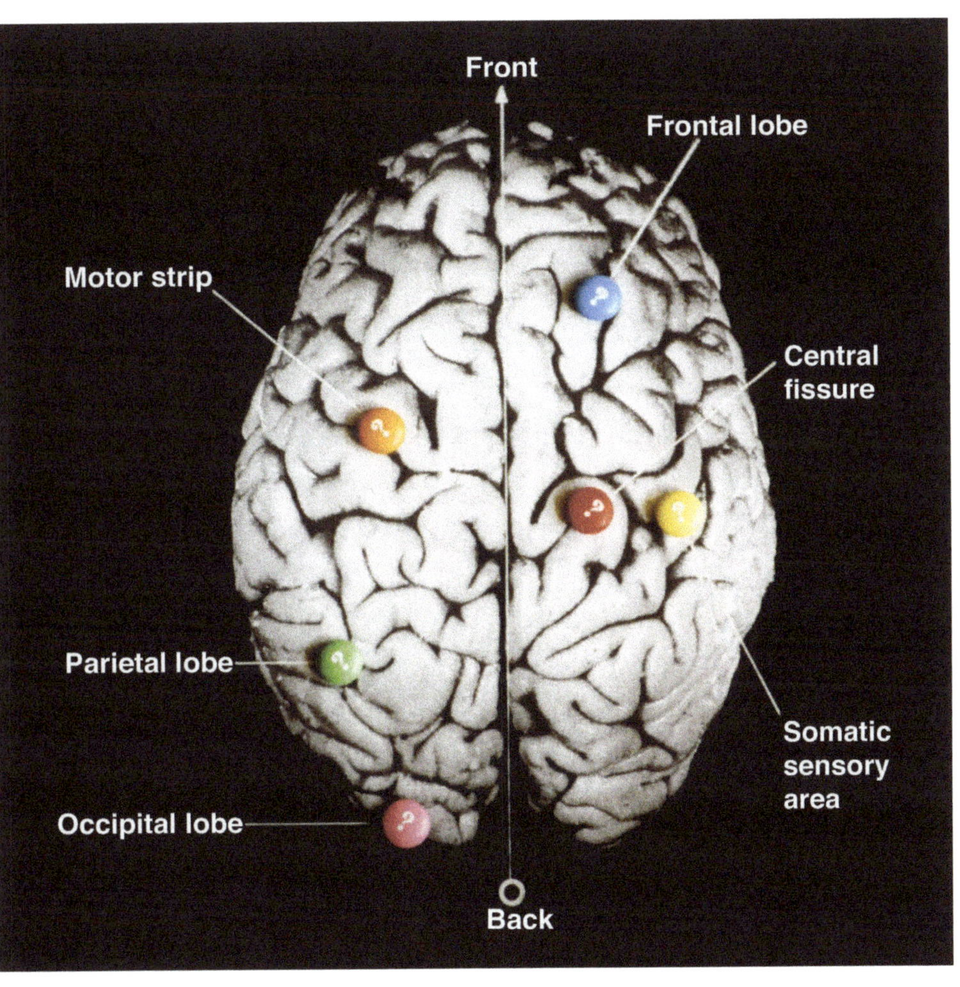

Front
Frontal lobe
Motor strip
Central fissure
Parietal lobe
Somatic sensory area
Occipital lobe
Back

Section 3: Twilight Zone

And so my mind, bedazzled and amazed,
stood fixed in wonder, motionless, intent,
and still my wonder kindled as I gazed.

Alighieri Dante [AD 1265-1321] - Mystical Poet

Winged Messenger

Summer time in an English country garden at my home in the north east. Church bells ringing, flowers blooming, bees buzzing. I was taking it all in, then I heard a voice, an auditory transmission that told me:

'You will receive true enlightenment when a butterfly settles on your head.'

Immediately I positioned myself close to a buddleia bush and watched from the corners of my eyes, willing and anticipating every passing butterfly to land on my head... I waited in vain.

Coincidently, a week later, my parents invited me to visit a butterfly sanctuary. Enthusiastically I accepted.

The glass house was teeming with life. Exotic butterflies everywhere, all the colours of the rainbow. I wandered through the heat and humidity of the simulated tropical forest certain that I was meant to be here, at this time, in this place, for one reason only. Again, my expectations were unfulfilled.

Two years later, just before daybreak, I entered the bathroom that backs on to my garden and found a peacock butterfly against the wall, trembling wings exposed. Reassuring her that she would be safe in my hands, I enveloped her and took her outside to greet the dawn. I opened my cupped hands and released her into the fresh air. She flew, spiraling upwards, then descended and settled securely on the crown of my head ... if enlightenment is joy, I was at that moment, a truly enlightened man.

Take 2

Late spring 2005. I received a telephone call from a Channel 4 programme researcher who explained that he was working on a television documentary exploring the spiritual dimension of *voice hearing*. He asked if I would be willing to participate in the film and requested I share some personal experiences.

I chose to tell him the story about the butterfly that settled on my head, preceded by the dictionary definition of the word *Psyche*. As I relayed the anecdote a peacock butterfly flew into the room. Delighted and surprised I exclaimed:

'Oh! A butterfly has just entered the room.'

'Has it?' responded the researcher emitting doubtful incredulity…

That was the last I heard from Channel 4.

Radiohead

A lazy sunny afternoon in Derbyshire. I strolled to a local shop to buy a cool beer. On my way I tried to recall a 1960s song - *Waterloo Sunset* … the melody eluded me.

Moments later, queuing at the counter, over the shop radio a presenter Introduces:

'Waterloo Sunset, The Kinks, a blast from the past.'

I walk home, beer in hand, happily whistling a now familiar tune …

Pop music of the spheres.

Me and My Shadow

New Year's Eve 1999, I sat by the fire and considered what the new millennium may hold for humankind. I combined my hands to form the shape of a butterfly, then rotating my wrists I created its mirror image, an eagle, a configuration remembered from childhood when casting shadows on my bedroom wall.

A voice communicated:

'The Butterfly and the Eagle ... this is the lesson.'

I pondered - we can choose the way of the butterfly or the way of the hawk, and that choice is literally in our hands.

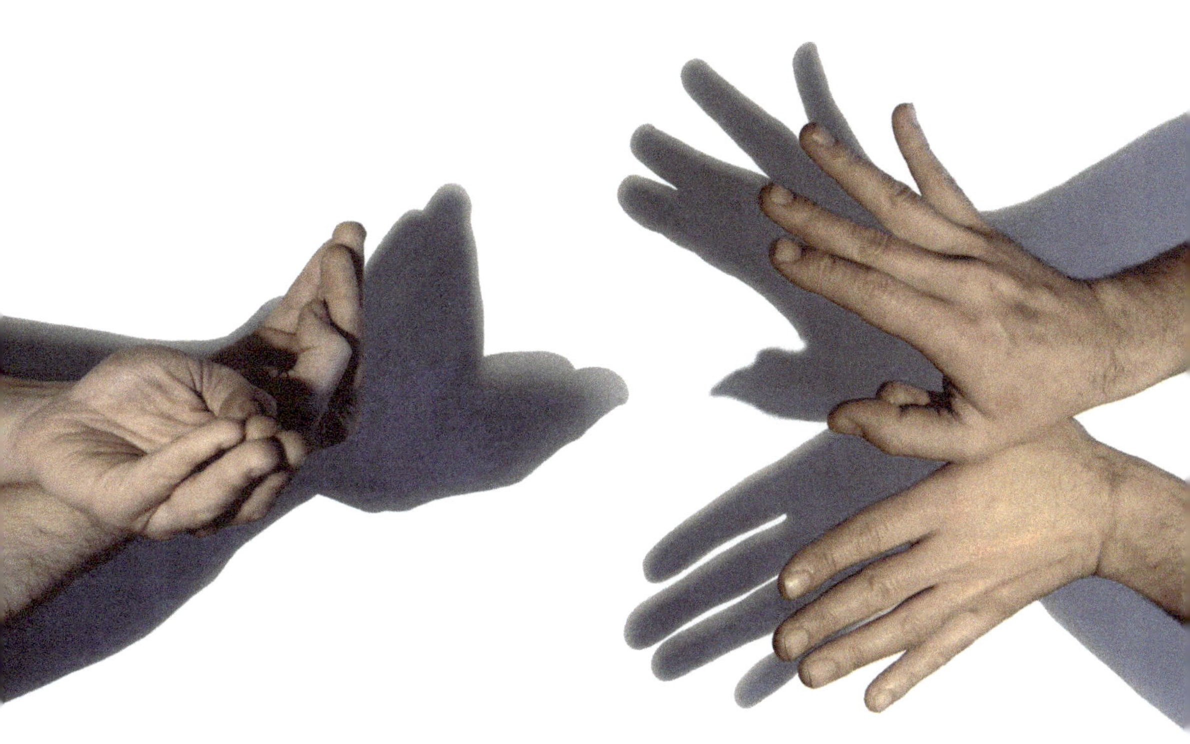

Hidden Depths

As I observed the constellation Orion my thoughts turned to the pyramids of Egypt and a question arose:

Why don't the pyramids shift in the sand?

An auditory transmission conveyed the words:

'As above, so below.'

A series of connecting lines flashed onto the night sky; a diagram of white light written in the stars, forming an *Octahedron.*◆

The question was answered. This vision, this voice, seemed to be revealing that the exposed pyramids are only half the story; that beneath their foundations, seated deep within the desert sand, like a diamond set in a ring, lies the other half waiting to be uncovered.

◆ *Red/Blue 3D Vision Glasses required to view Octahedron: Six points and eight equilateral triangles, utilised in Sacred Geometry, traditionally represents the element of air.*

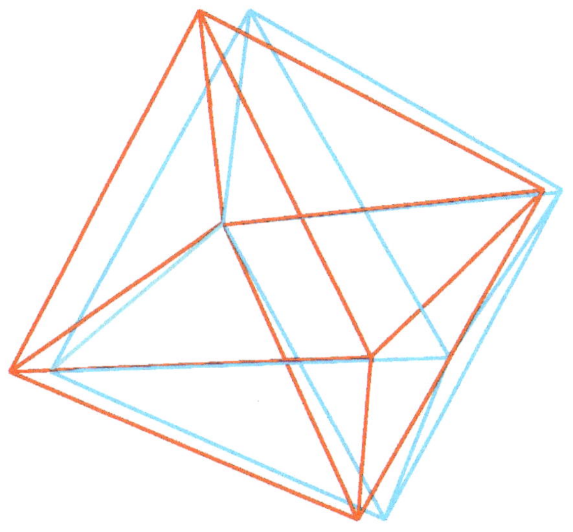

Visitor

Laying on my sofa one night listening to Erik Satie Gymnopédie, I fell into a deep sleep with a Jesus College Cambridge tie of red and black around my neck [wishful thinking as not a university in the land would have accepted me!].

I was woken at some point during the night by a woman with long golden hair.

In greeting she raised a hand, introduced herself as Sylvie, and spoke the words:

'Salvē.'

Then placing the silk fabric between thumb and forefinger said:

'Nice tie.'

After rising in the morning, I asked my father, Donald, who had a passion for linguistics, what the word Savlē meant? Da told me that the word is a greeting, with Latin roots, meaning Hello or Hail, and that in Roman times it was used as a command 'Be well!'.

I have no explanation for this visitation.

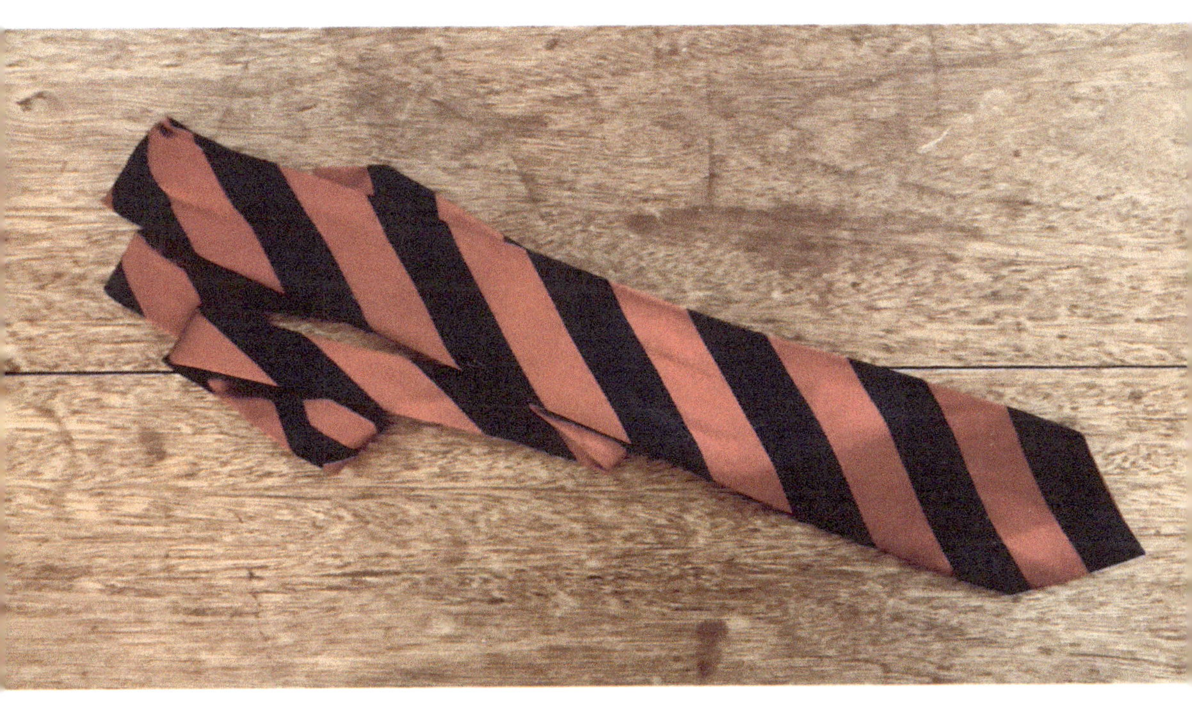

The Power of Words

As I approach my parents' house I see a rolled up newspaper at the foot of a local council litter bin. The voice once again makes its presence felt with the words:

'This is a test.'

I unroll the newspaper, a copy of The Sun, like a sacred scroll.

On the front page is the photograph of an ordinary man with the headline:

'MONSTER!'

The accompanying story reveals the man is a convicted serial paedophile.

I place a healing hand on the face of the Demon and put the newspaper in the bin.

The voice states:
'You have passed the test.'

Later that day something inside snaps.

I climb the stairs to the bedroom at the top of the house and reach into my father's wardrobe to remove his black shirt, with the intention of setting it alight.

A clearly audible hissing breathing emanates from the closet.

Unfased, I take the shirt downstairs, remove a copy of Mein Kampf [first edition] from my dad's book shelf [Da was no Nazi but he adored books], walk through the gate at the bottom of the garden, hang the shirt on the railings that border Langley Beck, and set fire to it. Opening the book, I kiss the portrait of Adolf Hitler printed on the inside page, throw it into the embers and watch it ignite.

My father was furious, asserting:

'When people burn books it's the end of civilisation!'
I countered:

'It's when people write books like this, that civilisation is under threat.'

We were both right and were forced to agree with each other.

The most bold and impactful printed advertisement I have seen, was a full page spread in a Sunday supplement promoting Waterstones. It depicted a chard book alongside the caption:

'Hitler was right about one thing ... the power of words.'

When the Saints go Marching in

August of 1997, Da had just passed away, and *One in a Hundred* was being staged at Durham Cathedral [where the remains of St. Aidan are entombed].

My girlfriend Tricia, who I was later to marry, had travelled from Derbyshire to console me and to see the show. During her visit she asked if I had ever been to the home of Saint Aidan - Holy Island in Northumberland.

I said 'No.'

'Then I shall take you there.'

When the exhibition came to a close, had been dismantled and put into store, we headed to Holy Island for a couple of nights. We returned from the island on August 31st - St. Aidan's Day. Back home I turned on the radio. The airwaves were dominated by the breaking news that Princess Diana had been killed in a car crash in Paris.

The Princess of Wales died on St. Aidan's Day, the date that commemorates the death of the Celtic Saint... DIANA is an anagram of AIDAN.

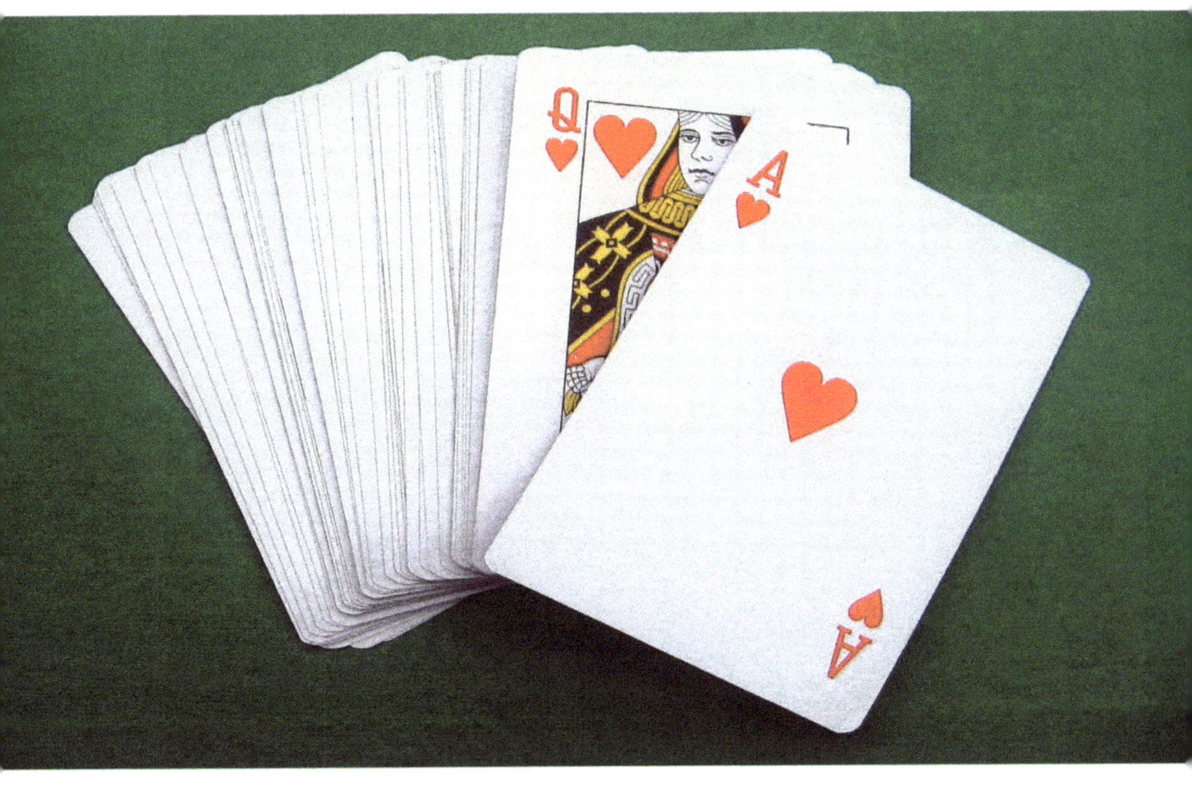

Jeepers Creepers

On the 16th April 1995, the people of Britain were told that it was 'PH**ONE**DAY'. The digit **1** was introduced into the existing area codes of the nation's telephone numbers; all area codes would now begin **01.** We were informed that this was required to:

'meet an increase in demand for numbers' and to
'create a more flexible code structure for the future.'

One evening in 1998 a voice transmitted:

'Dial 01 and ask for Blue Eyes - he hears, he sees, he taps, he spies.'

I picked up the telephone and dialled 01. Two minutes of silence was followed by a high pitched alarm emitting from the receiver. I replaced the handset then redialled. This time, it took around five minutes for the alarm to sound. The duration between first and second alarm was inconsistent. I dialled a third time, yet another timing anomaly.

Taking the experiment a stage further, I rigged up a sound system next to the telephone. Again, I lifted the handset and dialled 01, this time I played one of my Father's records:

Permission to Sing Sir by Clive Dunn of *Dad's Army* fame.

No alarm - it became clear I was being received. I gathered my own record collection and sent messages down the line until daylight. I said everything I have ever wanted to communicate to the state via music and song like a rebellious DJ.

Any doubt about the significance of the information imparted to me by the voice was removed the following night when I repeated my actions, then crept into bed beside Tricia who was sleeping.

We were woken during the early hours of the morning by the doorbell, the room pulsating with blue light and our dog barking frantically. I was greeted at the front door by two police officers who introduced themselves, then enquired,

'You're experiencing difficulties with your telephone?'

'I know why you are here; I will send no more messages.'
I answered.

The officers stepped back into their vehicle and drove away.

Next day, Tricia and Elizabeth [my mother] were perplexed and resolved to contact the police to find out why they had come to the house. My own attempts to explain the circumstances and events that had led to the police visit only served to fuel confusion and inflame disquiet. My mother was informed:

'We came to your house because we received what appears to be a silent 999 call.'

In subsequent years my telephone conversations have been punctuated by extraneous sounds plainly intended to make me aware that I am not alone. For example, one of the records I had sent down the telephone line was at a later date played back to me on my answer machine accompanied by a police radio transmission:

Alpha-Bravo-Charlie-Delta-Echo

I surmise the **01** code was introduced to facilitate an integrated and centralised telecommunication monitoring system and that 'Blue Eyes' is the code name ascribed to controller of operations, and I am left with the words *Paranoid Schizophrenia* ringing in my ears.

Honest to God

Having withdrawn from anti-psychotic drugs, I'm literally crying out for sanctuary.

I go to my local church, St. Mary's in Staindrop, County Durham.

At the atrium I hear a voice:

'Be honest to God, stand naked before the cross.'

I walk through the nave until I reach the altar, position myself behind it, take off my clothes, fold them neatly and place them on an adjacent pew. I then face the cross and succumb to trance.

Unbeknown to me, four German tourists enter the church, then beat a hasty retreat to report what they've just witnessed to the shop keeper in the newsagent across the road.

Shortly after I hear another voice:

'Aidan, this is not appropriate, this is a house of God.'

I open my eyes to find the curate and a member of the congregation standing before me. I declare:

'You are a man of the cloth, you're covered up. I'm standing naked before the cross, tell me which of us is being true to God?'

The two men leave the church and me with my maker in my birthday suit. It's not long before I'm joined by my mother, who with a wry smile, says:

'Look darling, you can remain here as you are until the men in white coats come to take you away, or you can put your clothes back on, come home with me, and have a cup of tea and biscuit … now which is it to be?'

Rather sensibly I choose the latter.

Seven for a Secret

My eyes focused on the glow of a candle flame. As I stare, moving images form, an inner vision appears and entering a *virtual reality* I embark upon an extraordinary journey of discovery ...

I'm overlooking a white marble staircase, I descend to a hall. On my left, a door with a spy hole. I pass through and find myself in a corridor. Immediately to my right another door. I enter to find a small room lined wall to wall, floor to ceiling, with grey safe deposit boxes; each is numbered.

A voice instructs me to open safe number seven with a key. This I do. I remove a plain rectangular box made of dark wood. I lift its lid; inside are three rusty nails, an ancient hammer and a false base, which I displace to uncover a single thorn on a remnant of sack cloth.

Puzzled, I asked: 'where am I?'

The voice informs me that I am in the Vatican; the words are proceeded by a stream of additional information.

I recite the transmission aware that by doing so I could expose myself to accusations of 'the ramblings of a mad man' and historical inaccuracy ...

- *The Pharisee originated from the Pharaoh.*

- *The Pharaoh punished the disobedient by crucifixion.*

- *The crucifix was designed and constructed on the principles of the 'golden section' - Sacred Geometry.*

- *The Pharaoh and the Pharisee ruthlessly guarded the secrets of Sacred Geometry and Mystical Knowledge from the people.*

- *Jesus of Nazareth denounced the Pharisee, demanding the priesthood reveal the secret knowledge they concealed.*

- *Jesus was crucified by the Pharisee for defying the priesthood.*

- *After the crucifixion of Jesus, the Pharisee sought to protect their interests by extending and increasing its power and influence to the seat of the Roman Empire. Over time an emerging and burgeoning Christian movement amassed to oppose the Pharisee. To placate and deflect the challenge to its authority the Pharisee became the Roman Catholic Church and established the Vatican State.*

- *Jesus' mission and message was subverted by the Catholic Church; He posed a serious threat to the Pharisaic Priesthood and for his sins was crucified. In his absence he was made 'High Priest' of the Catholic Church the Pontiff's puppet. The Pharisee is cloaked in Christianity.*

- *When Cardinals assemble and sit in Conclave to elect and initiate a new Pope, they do so on the basis that they are confident that the incumbent will guard the Vatican's secrets.*

- *The Pope is sworn to secrecy on his inauguration and entrusted with the key to Vatican City.*

- *The key to Vatican City opens all doors within the Vatican.*

- *The ancient relics revealed in safe deposit box seven were taken from Calgary to Rome after the crucifixion of Jesus of Nazareth. The wooden box was fashioned by Joseph, from the cross that Jesus was nailed to, and was crafted on the principle of the 'golden section'. The thorn on sack cloth is the thorn in the side of the Catholic Church.*

- *Within the room in which the safe deposit boxes are installed, there exists a wealth of ancient knowledge, including manuscripts confiscated by the Pharisee, written in Jesus' hand. In addition, the room contains material concerning humanity's history and origins.*

Six years after this experience at home, flicking through a copy of *The Guardian* newspaper dated 10th April 2004. On page 8, a photograph; an image of the very same scene I'd witnessed. The picture had been taken from a magazine titled 'Veja' and was reproduced in *The Guardian* along with a caption that read:

'An Easter message: receive the world at your door.'

There it was; the corridor and the door to the right that led to the room with the safe deposit boxes, plus an additional fixture - Pope John Paul II peering through the fish eye spy hole whilst holding up a crucifix to camera. I knew this place inside out.

A sense of foreboding impelled me to look up from the newspaper. Smack! Into the window pane flew a magpie! The bird lay stunned on the window sill. Startled, I reflected and considered the significance... magpie indeed.

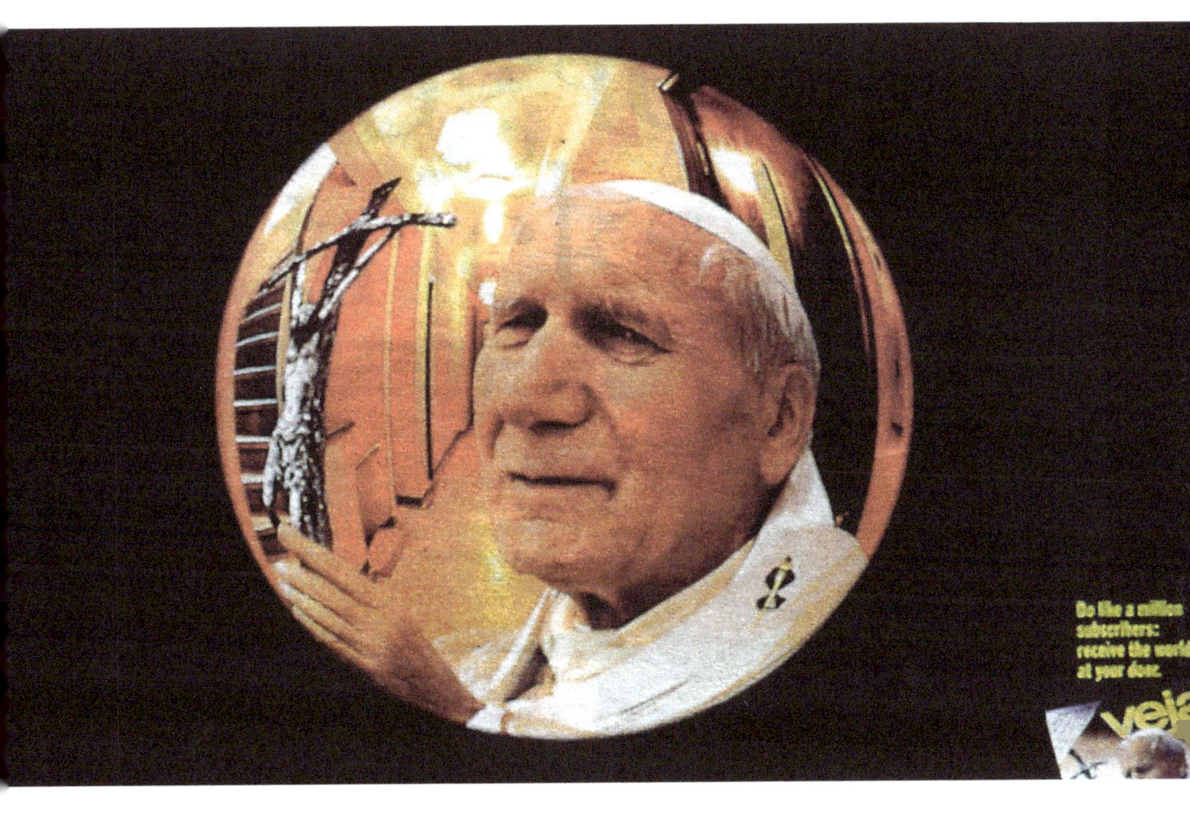

Do like a million
subscribers:
receive the world
at your door.
veja

Encounter

The sky was awash with stars as I walked my dog on a snow-covered village green in County Durham. I looked to the heavens with wonder and voiced a request; an invitation to the Star People, the beings that we describe as extraterrestrials:

'If you would like to reveal yourselves, I would be very happy to receive you.'

Returning to my house, dog at my side, I looked eastwards beyond the main street, and there passing slowly and silently through space, leaving a trail of golden light in its wake was a huge radiant green sphere; a luminous emerald orb, which descended to Earth and appeared to land in pastures a few hundred yards from me.

Overflowing with gratitude, two words passed my lips…'Thank you.'

Star Child

I was compelled to buy over £300 worth of merchandise from a local shop. The brand names of the items I'd acquired possessed significance: Galaxy chocolate bars, Honey Nut Loops breakfast cereal, Bold Automatic washing powder, Signal toothpaste, and so on. Amongst this array of shopping, a solitary Kinder Surprise egg.

An auditory transmission had conveyed there was to be an encounter with *Celestial Beings* that night. The voice instructed me to take the products I had purchased along with four reflective spires I'd constructed previously, to fields just outside the village. The voice indicated that the goods were to be offered as a gift for the visitors.

I arrived at the rendezvous point at midnight full of anticipation. During the early hours I received a further communication:

'Within the egg there is a Star Child waiting to be born.'

I placed the Kinder Surprise egg under one of the spires.

No encounter took place that night. The morning however, brought the farmer whose land I was on, his father, the farmer's wife, at the same time, my parents and a friend who took a sequence of photographs with my camera. After reassuring the farmer I intended no harm, I told the gathering about the egg and what the voice had communicated.

I then opened the chocolate egg to release the surprise. Inside, I found a small plastic effigy of the children's cartoon character Asterix. Unaware of its bearing, I laughed dismissively and wrote the incident off as a whacky aberration.

It was not until a later date, when I relayed the whole story to my brother, that I was truly surprised… he told me that Asterix means Star!

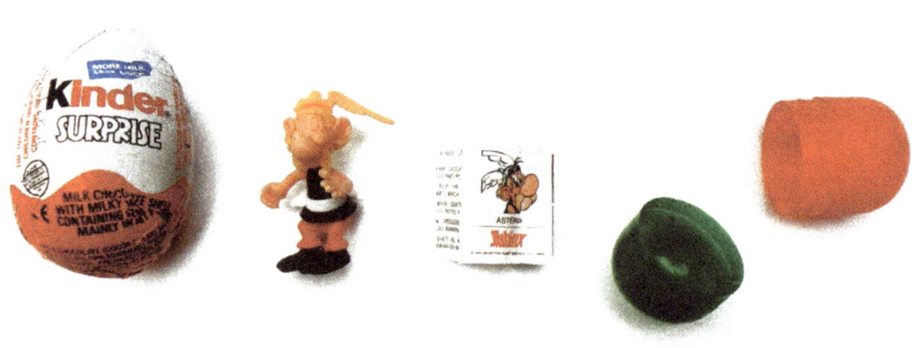

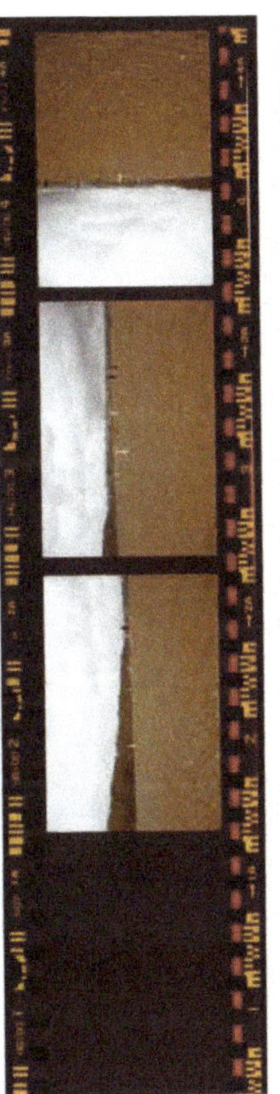
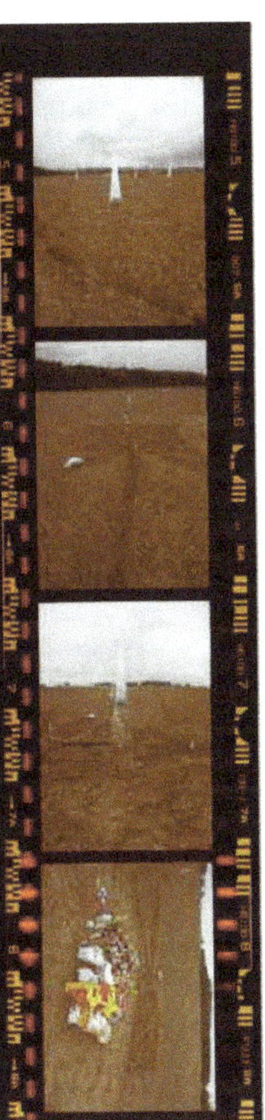
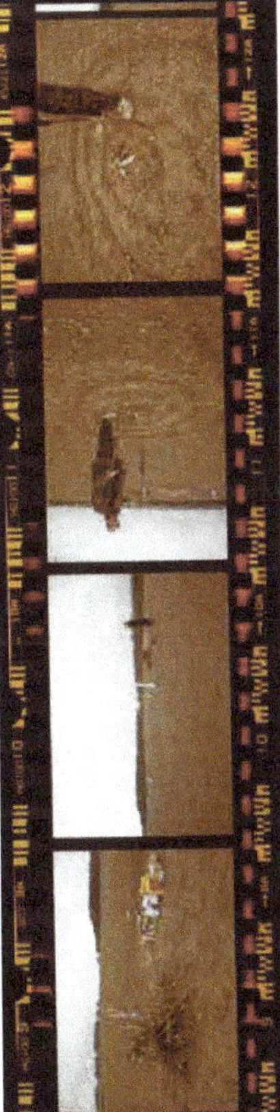
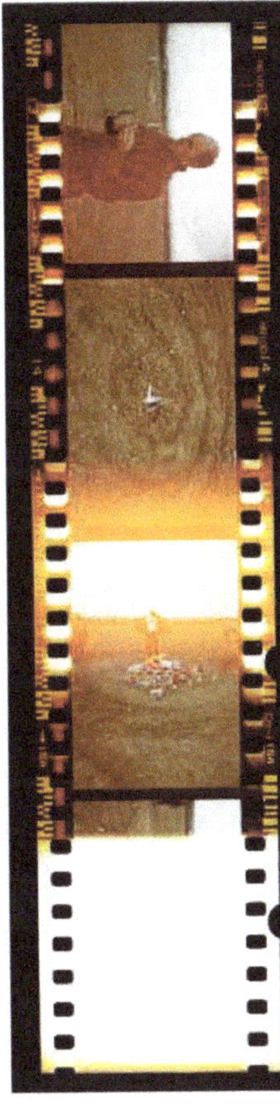

An aside to this tale is that I accidentally opened the back of the camera exposing the film to daylight. The prospect of losing the photographic record was disappointing. Again the voice spoke to reassure me not to worry, but to seek the light when the photographs had been developed - this was the final exposure…

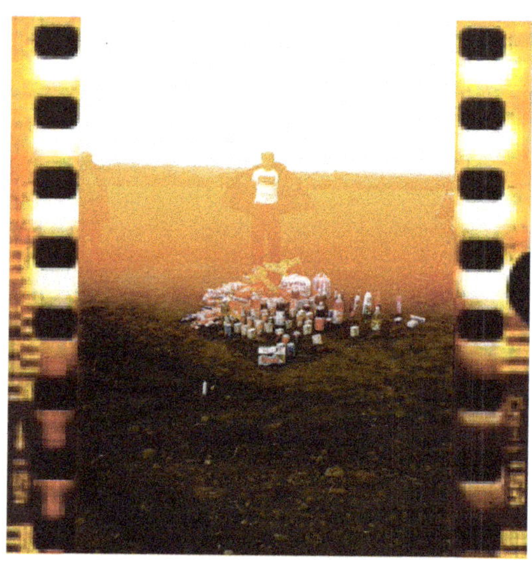

Section 4: Voice of Sanity

They told me that the night and day were all that I could see,
they told me that I had five senses to enclose me up,
and they enclosed my infinite brain into a narrow circle,
and sank my heart into the abyss.

William Blake -18th Century Visionary Artist

The Emperor's New Clothes

The term *Schizophrenia* was contrived in 1912 by
Professor Eugen Bleuler, a Swiss psychiatrist … *Clever Dick!*

Schizo - [Greek] - **split**
Phrene - [Greek] - **mind**

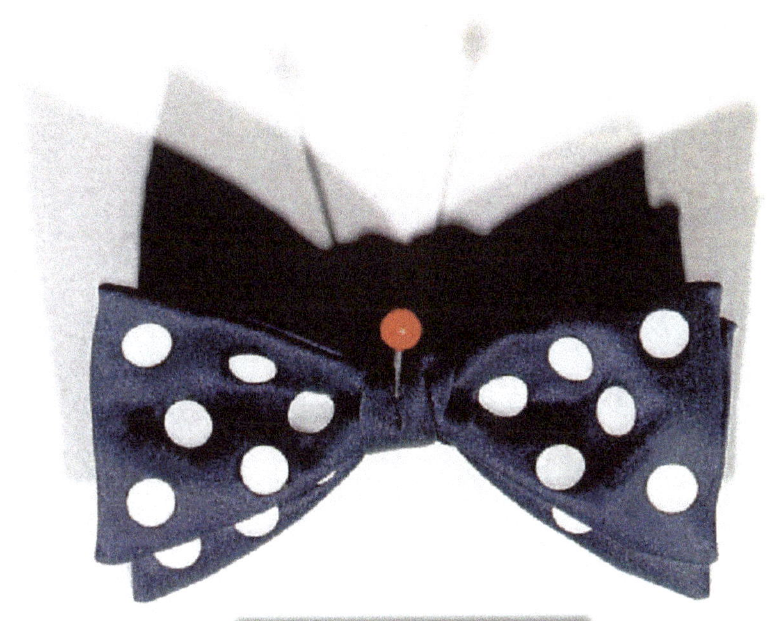

Prof. Eugen Bleuler, Psych.
(1857-1939)

People in Glass Houses

April 1998: A doctor paid a visit to my house to gauge my state of mind. Following a fractious discussion I told him, in no uncertain terms, to leave. I'd withdrawn from neuroleptic drugs. For years I'd been prescribed *Haloperidol;* the side effects were intolerable, inducing *Pseudoparkinsonism,* accompanied by an impending risk of *Tardive-dyskinesia* [an irreversible disfiguring disorder causing uncontrollable involuntary movements of the face, neck, tongue, fingers and limbs]. Now I was experiencing cold turkey and resisting psychiatric intervention.

Soon after they were hammering on the back door:

'Mr Shingler, Mr Shingler... open up!'

I was not going to let them in.

Then I heard the sound of wood splintering as the lock was prised off and the door forced open. They charged in, four police officers, a team of paramedics, social workers and a psychiatrist.

I was first taken to a police cell, and then the institution. I was tracked by a wall-mounted surveillance camera as I entered the asylum and ushered to an examination room where my physical and mental state was tested and assessed. The examining doctor asked if I was psychic, if I heard voices and had visions. Unwisely I said 'yes'. Six pink pills were placed in the palm of my hand: Haloperidol 60mg. I was instructed to swallow. I was shown to a hospital bed - the bedclothes were imprinted with the words *'Health Authority'*. Thus began a period of eight weeks incarceration; detained under Section 3 of the Mental Health Act.

I attempted to orientate myself to a hostile and alien environment. I was placed on 'Ten-minute Obs', which meant I was confined to the ward, my behaviour observed and recorded around the clock at ten-minute intervals. Throughout the night my sleep was intermittently broken by a shadowy figure on ward round who would enter and shine a torch directly in my face.

The shabby dayroom was a communal space in which an endless stream of caffeine and nicotine were consumed - there was nothing else to do and nowhere else to go. Friendships formed between patients. A deep sense of connection existed between us in the face of adversity; a gallows humour prevailed.

Some of my fellow inmates had black circles the size of old pennies seared into their temples; marks caused by the high voltage current that ran to the terminals attached to the head during electric shock treatment. I learned that those undergoing such treatment were frequently forced to do so.

The 'Electro-Convulsive Therapy' chamber was located in the centre of the ward. Also situated on the ward, an 'Observation Room,' in which a two-way mirror was installed.

The rattle of pill bottles heralded 'Medication Time' as the drugs dispenser was routinely wheeled through the ward. We were rounded up and regimented in queues to receive our prescribed dosage four times daily. The administering of drugs began at 8 a.m. and continued to 10 p.m. I refused to accept their tablets.

In the first week I witnessed three of my new friends being dragged to the 'Seclusion Room' to be forcibly injected.

By the end of that week I was convinced every mirror in the hospital was a two-way mirror and that everywhere eyes were watching me. I feared I was next in line to have my brain wired up and be electrocuted. I felt threatened by the imminence of being forcibly drugged. I perceived the institution as a Nazi concentration camp and the staff as guards. I was also incensed at the inhumanity of a system that was cruelly failing my compatriots and myself at a time when our vulnerability and volatility should have been cradled and protected.

It was at this point the head of the Department of Psychiatry analysed me and insisted I take the drugs. I enquired: 'why?'

'Because I think you are ill.' came the reply.

On hearing these words clinically induced paranoia and fury collided; I lashed out and punched the psychiatrist in the face. Immediately eight or so staff descended upon me as an alarm bell rang out. I was put in head and arm locks, pain compliance techniques were implemented, marched through a corridor to a cell, forced to the ground, stripped naked, my arse pierced with syringes, injected with a massive dose of neuroleptic drugs, and left, locked in the cell, utterly alone, terrified and traumatised, as I began to lose consciousness ... Medication Time ...

A Spoonful of Sugar

Antipsychotic drugs [also known as neuroleptics or major-tranquillisers] are powerful and complex substances. There is a vast amount yet to be understood about the intricate interplay and specific interactions of these drugs and their impact on the neurological system. I feel however, that they can fulfil a valuable role in assisting individuals in their quest for balance, but only if there is a balance of interests between those prescribing and those receiving. Lamentably the means and methods by which these drugs are systematically imposed by clinicians give rise to a profound conflict of interests.

I ascribe neuroleptics with alchemic properties, attributing them with the ability to act on the human *Psyche* in ways not yet grasped in pharmaceutical research laboratories. My reading is that schizophrenia is a psychic experience that manifests itself as spiritual unrest. The openness and susceptibility to the effects of *paranormal stimuli* by those undergoing *psyche-sensitivity* can be overwhelming; a dam burst causing a flash flood of psychic turbulence that fills the plains of the mind.

If neuroleptics are administered sensitively, then rather than suffocating psychic activity through chemical saturation, these compounds can function as a filter and possess the potential to limit the frequency and intensity of paranormal occurrences by reducing the *psychic aperture*, thereby enabling *psychic upsurge* to be channelled and assimilated. Used minimally, these drugs can improve rather than impoverish the lives of those on the receiving end.

All too often major-tranquillisers are administered as an overdose that nullifies the neurologic system rendering the recipient brain-dead. The expression less is more springs to mind. Antipsychotic drugs need not be a bitter pill to swallow.

Pins and Needles

Psychiatry has a shameful history and deplorably it has carried many aspects of that past into the present. Modern day psychiatry is certainly more sophisticated, but it is not necessarily more sensitive. In the battle to rid the world of states of consciousness that dare to stray beyond the bounds of possibility, clinicians have incorporated into their armoury a weapon that is used routinely and without qualms. It is an implement that inflicts a high dose of trauma and leaves emotional scars that never quite heal. The needles that are forced deep into the buttocks of those dragged to the 'Seclusion Room', pinned to the floor, stripped naked and left in a locked cell to recede into unconsciousness, pierces not only the flesh of its victims, but also their hearts; hearts that bleed long after the Elastoplasts have been removed. For the countless individuals who do not survive psychiatric assault [fatalities are not uncommon] an epitaph awaits…

Rest in Pieces.

Universal Declaration of Human Rights:

Article 5.

No one shall be subjected to torture or to cruel, inhuman or degrading treatment or punishment.

Split/Mind

Psychiatry's attempts to manipulate the manifestations of unusual states of consciousness to conform to, and comply with, a medical model, have had devastating consequences for the victims of those subjected to *Psychosurgery;* the current term for lobotomy and leucotomy - the severing or removal of parts of the brain. One could be forgiven for asking the question:

Who is the psycho?

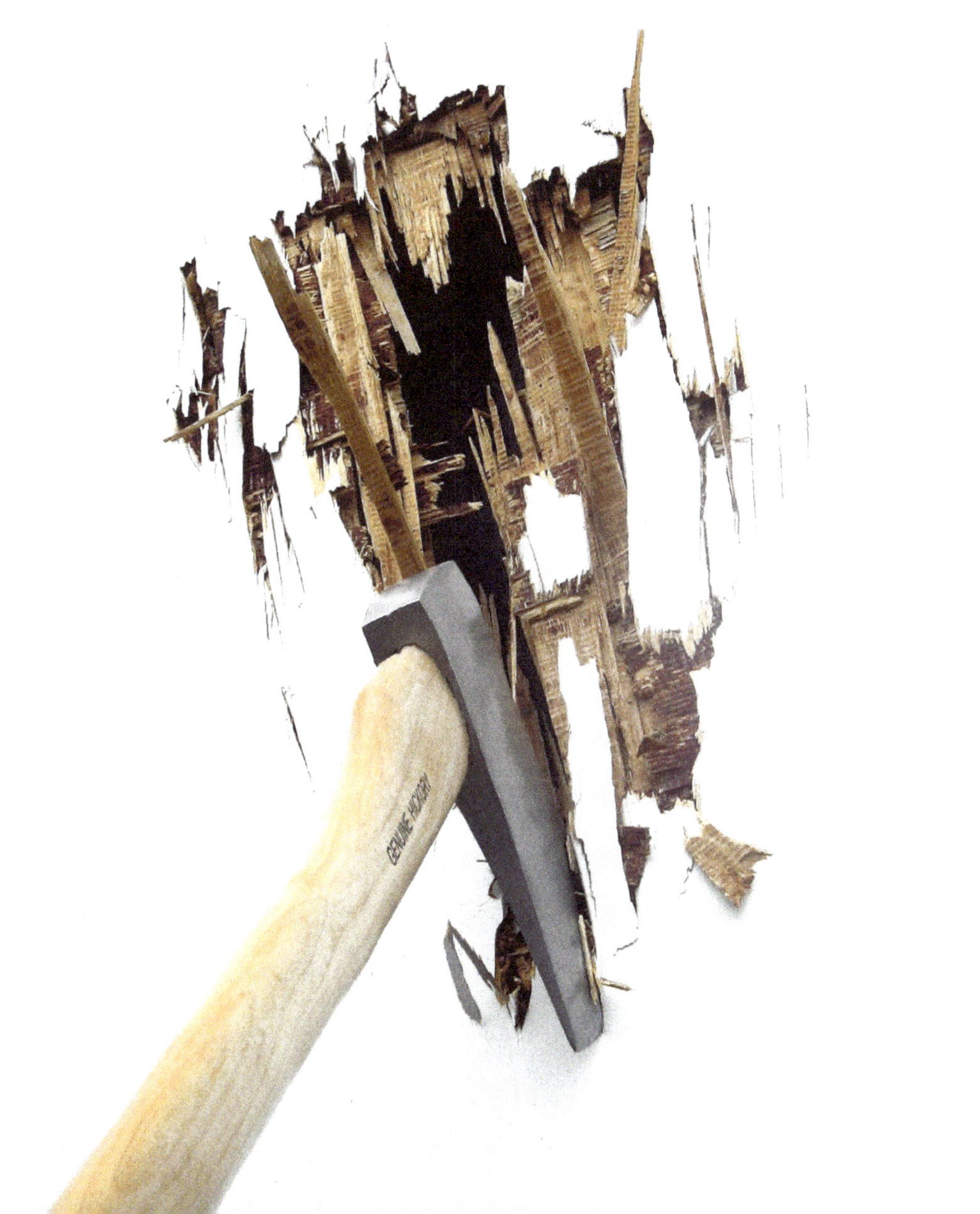
GENUINE HICKORY

Wired for Sound

I don't know the criteria by which clinicians regard voice hearing as a manifestation of psychological disorder - I do know that admitting to hearing voices is sufficient to be recorded and treated as a symptom. Quizzed by a psychiatrist about the nature and content of the voice I was hearing, I answered that it was an angelic voice communicating the words:

'Everything is going to be all right.'

The consultant muttered under his breath: 'Auditory hallucination.'

In truth, everybody hears voices, and they resonate in many forms. As I write these lines my thoughts are audibly formulating; I am hearing a voice loud and clear. As you read these words you are internalising my thoughts; you are hearing a disembodied voice communicating thoughts that are independent of yourself. Equally, do you not converse with yourself through audibly articulated thought; thoughts that are sometimes incompatible, indicating an aspect of your conscience is resistant to reason ... doctor's dilemma. Furthermore, we sleep, we dream. When we access our dream world, we enter into a union of intimate dialogue rich in meaningful metaphor; dialogue that assists us apprehend and resolve psychological predicaments. Dreams are the source of so much of humanity's inspired creativity. Dreams enrich our imagination and help shape our consciousness.

The means by which our inner being reveals itself to us is by voicing itself, echoing the many facets and complexities that define our individuality and humanity. Surely it is far more constructive and progressive to work creatively with voices.

The supernatural is natural... extrasensory perception is a reality.

What of those who receive audible transmissions understood to emanate from an aethereal or divine source? Those who channel and communicate mysterious words of wisdom, known to theology as locutions. What of those who hear the voice of a departed loved one? What of mediums? What of telepathic communications or clairaudience?

Psyche-sensitives often describe their voices using terms such as: transmissions, signals, broadcasts, frequencies, wavelengths, interference. When we do so, we are attempting to describe and substantiate a real phenomenon; the neurologist and the radio engineer speak the same language.

Are these phenomena to be written off as perceptual hallucinations symptomatic of psychological dysfunction? If so, and this is the crux - *the paranormal comes to mean the abnormal, the psychic becomes the psychotic, the unprovable becomes the impossible, and the infinite unknown is reduced and restricted to the monotony and pomposity of clinical certainty.*

The Test

Auditory transmissions can be profoundly disturbing, often voice hearers are challenged by intensely oppressive commands.

Religious scriptures of most faiths cite examples of moral discord arising from the monovalent edicts of aethereal annunciations. Their teachings convey the perils of obedience and the triumphs of resistance. The biblical fable of Jesus being led into the wilderness to be tempted by the devil is a case in point.

I too have had to contend with hostile voices but learned to quell their menace through discernment.

By reconciling and recognising transmissions as a *Test*, I've been able to regard voice hearing as a *Rite of Passage*, and become empowered to make wise choices, my conscience fortified as opposed to compromised.

With patience, compassion and vigilance, I've made peace with my shadow and in doing so gained a benign messenger.

It could be said that clairaudience is fortuitous, for without the benefit of the spoken word people may well be tested insidiously and remain oblivious to the unconscious dictates that influence their actions.

If psychiatrists were able to embolden, rather than inhibit individuals, to take control of, and responsibility for their voices, a true reciprocal partnership may develop; a mutually co-operative relationship which could equip each to accept the voice as a natural, inherent and genuine expression of human being - being human. Then perhaps, the voice might become the teacher... testing, testing 1,2,3.

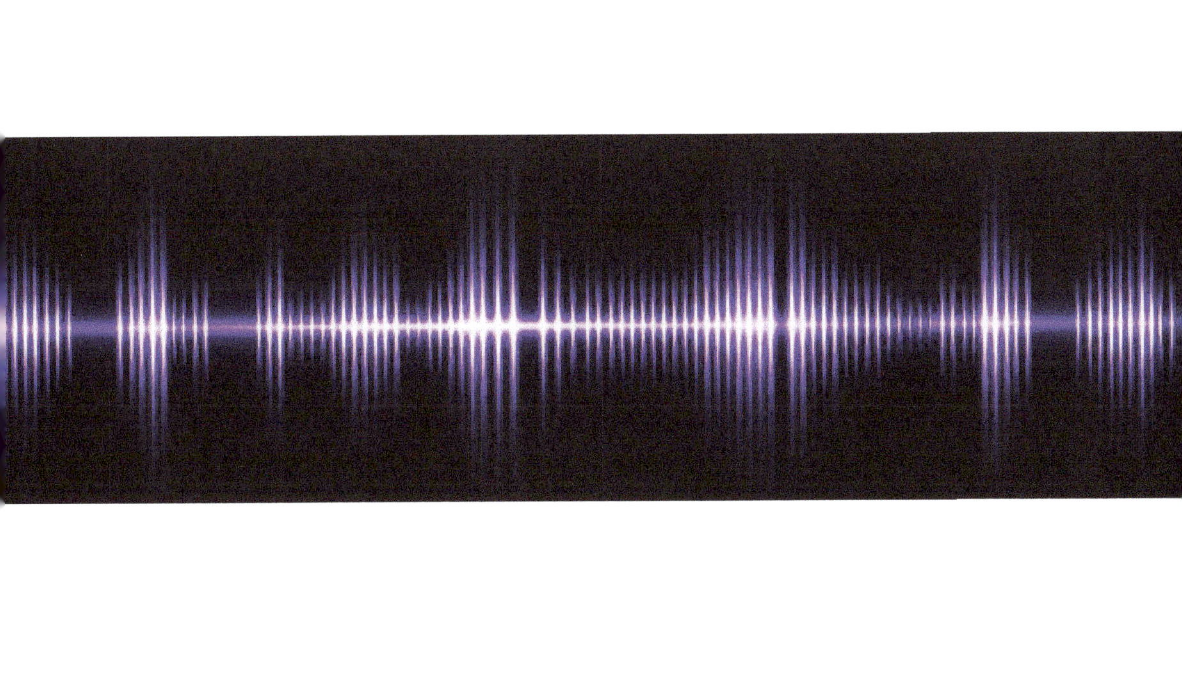

Advice for Smarties

Indelibly stamped upon my memory, not least because my humour was strangely unappreciated, is a presentation I was invited to give to a convergence of psychiatrists, at which I posed the following question:

What is the difference between God and a psychiatrist?
Answer: God does not believe he is a psychiatrist!

It is evident from my experience and from discourse with people who have been put through the psychiatric system, that there is an attempt to control, rather than care for, individuals experiencing unusual states.

Incarceration, physical restraints, pain compliance techniques, takedowns, forced drugging [acuphase], compulsory ECT, psychosurgery, brainwashing, demonstrates the defectiveness rather than the effectiveness of psychiatric treatment and equates with state sanctioned torture.

I counsel the psychiatric fraternity, rather than obliterate anomalous experiences, that you assist integrate them in into people's lives in a coherent, constructive and creative way. To undertake this requires you to be profoundly insightful and demands a comprehensive knowledge of the interplay of the light and dark forces which affect us all. This, in turn, necessitates you to be receptive to human spirituality and to acknowledge the authenticity of your patient's reality.

By '*pathologising*', '*symptomising*' and '*clinicising*' unusual states, psychiatrists debase, devalue, undermine and attempt to invalidate these experiences. This only serves to bewilder and exacerbate disturbance.

'*Judge-mental*' is a very revealing word.

Although 'schizophrenic rationale' does away with commonplace logic, reason is integral to this state of being but is encrypted in metaphor.

You may be given access to this code, but only if you open your hearts and minds and LISTEN. To appraise the *psyche-sensitive* you need to be aware that our experiences and perceptions are woven into the fabric of reality … believe it or not.

Rationalism is only one way of perceiving. It has a place, but not to the exclusion or detriment of the broad spectrum of thoughts and emotions that characterise the rich tapestry of the human experience.

The term *mental health* implies that our emotional well-being is determined by mental faculties or processes located in, and confined to the brain, somehow isolated or disconnected from the rest of our being, like a walnut rattling around the cave of the skull. Is this not the true 'split' that you, the clinicians, have made yourselves? The severing of mind and spirit. Mental health also evokes the converse, *mental unhealthiness,* which quite frankly, reeks of disinfectant!

Is the human condition itself to be regarded as a medical condition in urgent need of treatment?

I am reminded of my father's incisive definition of an expert:

'An expert is someone who knows more and more about less and less
and in the end knows everything about fuck all.'

Life is suffused with spirit; we are a unification of coexistent energies and elements, tangible and intangible. Our well-being is determined by our relationship to our whole being, by being whole, at One with Oneself.

The emphasis you the consultants, place on your patients' lack of insight, belies your own lack of insight. You project all you do not and cannot comprehend as *'psychiatric disorder'*. I counsel you further to accept the advice that one of your own fraternity once offered me:

'Take a long hard look at yourself in the mirror...'

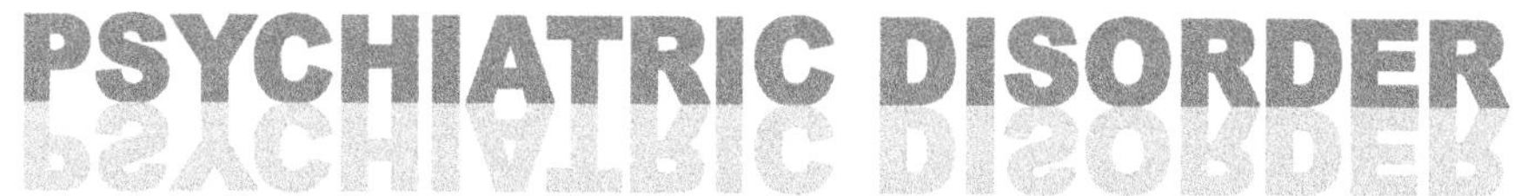

All you see reflected is all you have projected. You too are *'under observation'*.

I do not wish to condemn or hold in contempt those sincerely caring people who work within the current system, but if your calling was motivated by compassion, you should search your conscience. Human rights violations are endemic and epidemic within and throughout the psychiatric system; I urge you to convey what you have witnessed within your profession. For psychiatry to heal others it must first heal itself ✚

✚ **P A N E** - *Psychiatry A National Emergency.*

Section 5: Winds of Change

All in all we move as One,
We can find a way,
We will find a way,
A New World.

IO EARTH - 21st Century Symphonic Rock Band

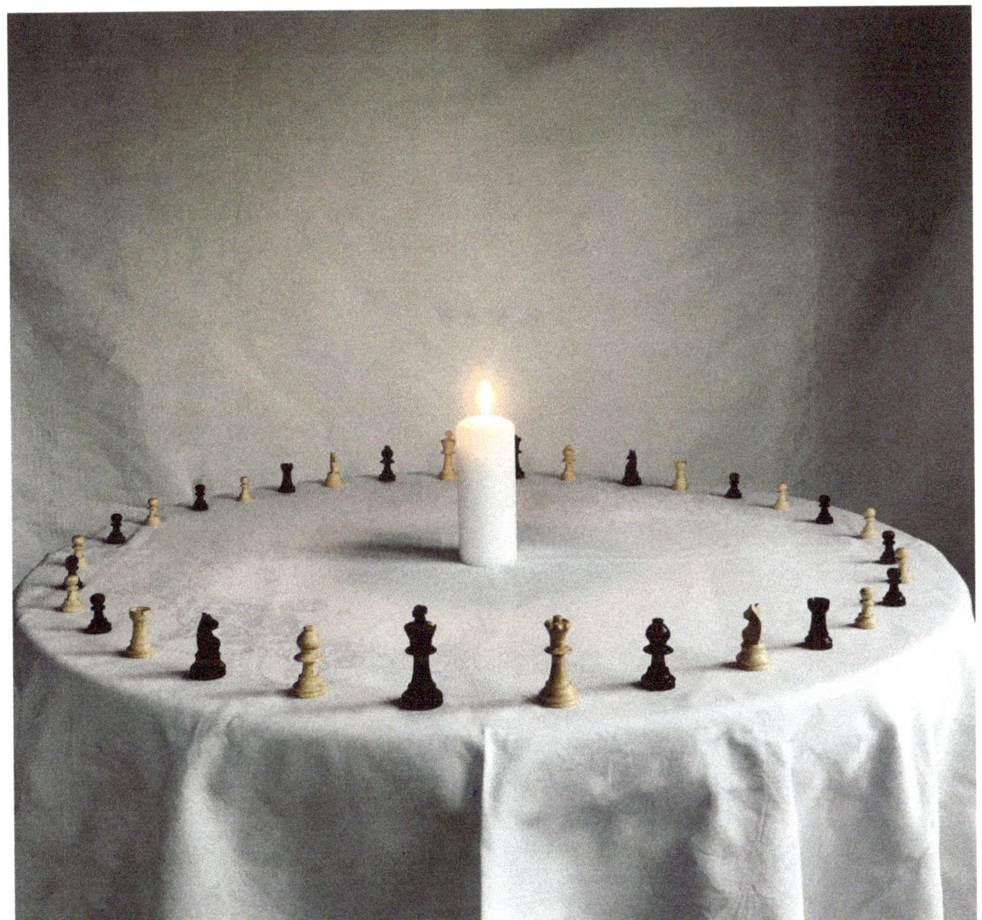

Power to the People

On Valentine's Day morning [Monday 14th Feb 2005], in partnership with my friend Catherine Ingram of Derbyshire Voice, the culmination of two years planning, and preparation came to fruition. Hundreds of survivors of the psychiatric system gathered at the City of Westminster's Whitehall in London with the shared aim of bringing the issue of *Psychiatric Assault* to the attention of the public, MP's and the media, and to urge radical reform of the mental health system; a protest against the abusive methods and practises employed by psychiatry which are endorsed and facilitated by the state.

Protesters applied injection plasters in the form of two ✖'s to their bums and marched past The Department of Health and Parliament, concluding at the Imperial War Museum [the original site of Bedlam asylum], where a rally was held, issues raised and testimonies heard.

En route, peaceful, poignant and humorous gestures of defiance were made; an 'in yer face' expression of outrage that mirrored back to the psychiatric establishment the disrespectful and humiliating treatment it imposes. I had titled the campaign:

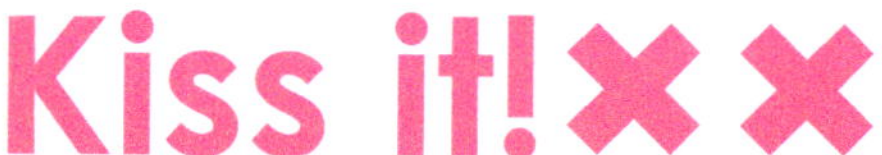

I, and a delegation, which amongst others included Dr Joanna Bennett, whose brother David had been disgracefully treated and tragically killed at the hands of psychiatry, delivered a petition and a Valentine's card that pin-pointed the issue to 10 Downing Street. The card, bearing the Prime Minister's name, was

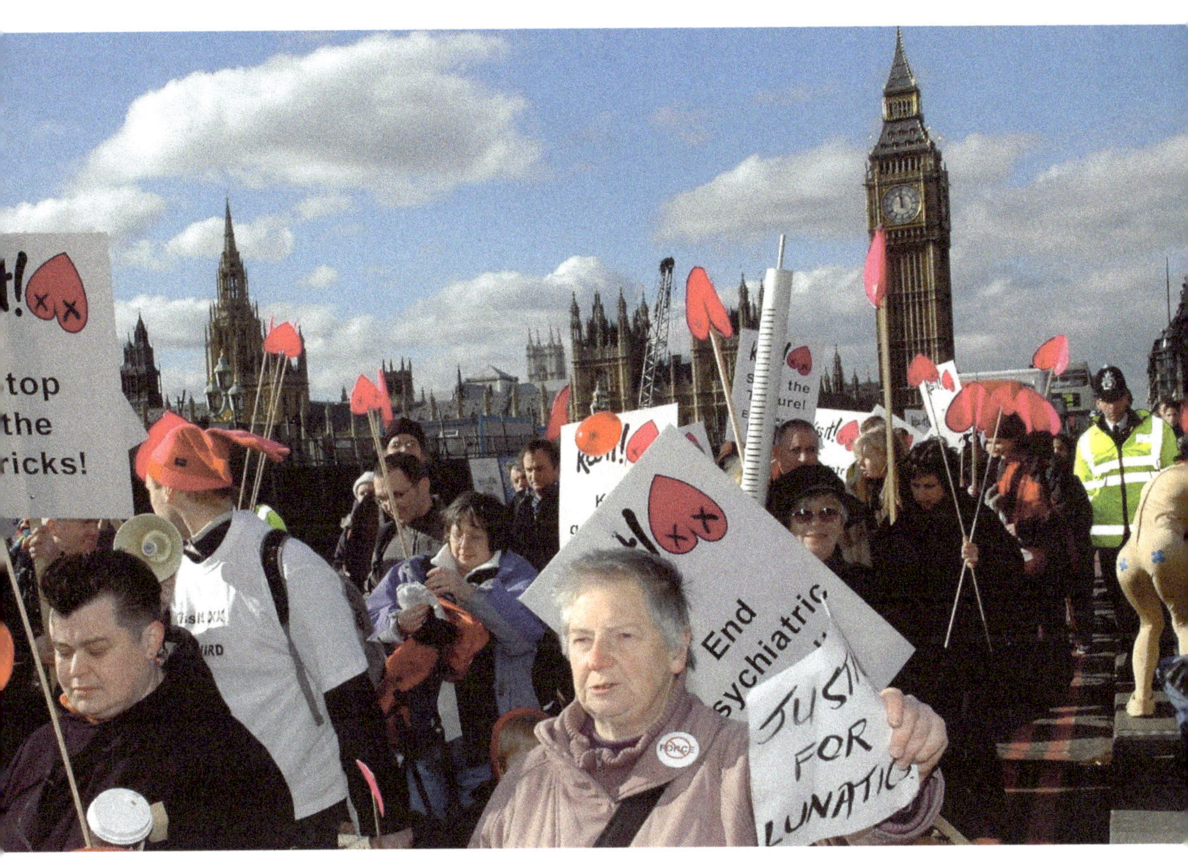

t!
top
the
ricks!
End
sychiatric
JUSTI
FOR
LUNATIC

intended to prick the government's conscience. It depicted, in true cupid fashion, a heart pierced by an arrow, but when the card was opened the heart was turned upside down to form an arse and the arrow became syringe. An accompanying message read:

Have a Heart ...

I trust the Prime Minster did not miss the point.

In addition to its obvious connotation, **Kiss it! ✖✖** also conveyed, *Kiss it Better* and *Kiss it Goodbye.* The two crosses represented ✖ *Marks the Spot, Double Crossed* and simply *Wrong!*

The changes that are so imperative, will I feel, come about when the covers are pulled back and the naked truth is exposed for all to see; a corrupt and incestuous relationship between psychiatry, the state and the drugs industry ... professional self-interest, the politics of social control and the colour of money, all rolled into one.

We should search for creative and imaginative solutions to replace the tyranny of the present regressive clinical regime. I look forward to the day when survivors of the psychiatric system become an organised Civil Rights Movement and our collective and united voice is heard and heeded. Maybe then, psychiatric oppression can be consigned to the history books.

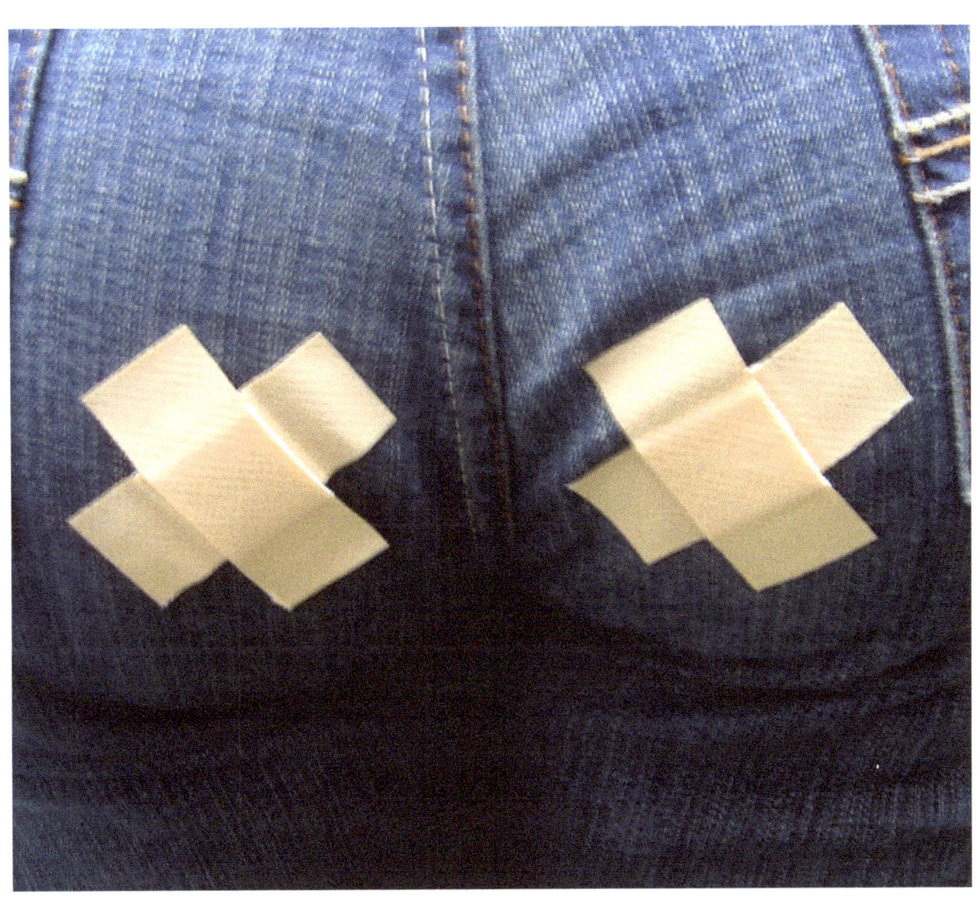

The Meaning of Life

Rapid developments in Genetic Engineering Technologies foreshadow further widespread, intensified medical intervention - the race to find the *schizophrenic gene* is underway. The debate as to whether there is a genetic predisposition to schizophrenia runs parallel. Setting aside the arguments and evidence for and against a link, imagine if such a gene were identified. It would certainly be regarded as a faulty gene, an abnormal mutation, undesirable in much the same way as schizophrenics are viewed in real life, and as in real life, the powers that be would undoubtedly attempt to prevent this trait finding expression. Would babies be weaned on neuroleptic drugs or maybe eugenics implemented? Mothers encouraged to terminate pregnancy or offered the opportunity to have offspring modified through gene editing; parents invited to make 'informed decisions' guided by specialists prone to produce and promote a *Sanitised World* - the imperfect schizophrenic deleted from the book of life.

Medical science is literally in our veins, are we also to allow it to enter and alter our genetic composition, to manipulate and contort the course of human evolution, to interfere with our destiny?

I was once told of an experiment that involved the premature extraction of a butterfly from its chrysalis, when the butterfly unfurled her wings, she was devoid of colour, a neutral grey.

Butterflies communicate across great distances. Entomologists presume that they do so by means of pheromones and that when a pair encounter each other, they engage in an adversarial 'dog fight'. My interpretation is very different, that antenna function as transmitters and receivers [why else would insects have aerials on their heads!] I see butterflies' summon each other, and in flight, I notice that their spiralling interplay forms a double helix, mimicking DNA ... they do not duel, they dance; the code of life on display for all who care to see.

Could we not create a climate in which we value and validate the acute perceptiveness of the *psyche-sensitive*, and celebrate such states as clear and unmistakable evidence of humankind evolving here and now, unfolding before us?

Should we not embrace and encourage, rather than despise and fear, the potential we possess as sentient beings to explore and experience the labyrinths of our *Psyches*? For only by doing so, can we make new discoveries, learn about ourselves and each other, be free to see our true colours, and realise our true selves.

Rhyme and Reason

Ask yourself this question:

Would the state of Israel, the United Nations, UNESCO, NATO, democracy in Germany, the formation of the European Union, Universal Declaration of Human Rights, an era of relative global peace and prosperity, have come into being if it were not for WW2?

Now ask yourself, where else in life and history does this principle of cause and effect apply?

Is there a hidden agenda that we may be privy to, if we free ourselves from ridged thinking, preconceptions and judgementalism?

Could it be that atrocities, in their many guises, are orchestrated by an invisible hand, perversely required to deliver healing, love, connection and deep bonds between families, friends, individuals, communities, nations?

How else can humanity develop and advance with insight, understanding, forgiveness and collective compassion?

Shared adversity presents an opportunity to bring people together through shared purpose ... united we stand.

Do we all perform a role, allocated or chosen for or by us before birth, in order to facilitate the greater good?

I see truth as a crystal clear multi-faceted cut stone. As the gem catches the light and catches the eye, one can convince oneself that the beguiling lens flare is the one true light, and become fixated on the purity and brilliance that particular aspect. Those that observe the stone from a different angle will be equally convinced that it is they who see the light. To me, it is the jewel itself, with its kaleidoscope of perspectives, that is the whole truth.

Call of the Stars

In the lead up to Christmas 2021, I was exposed to a torrent of *Precognition* and *Psychic Insight* which no amount of medication could suppress. *Cosmic Luminosity* was revealed to me after putting pen to paper with the following italicized paragraphs:

'If past, present and future, abide in the Eternal Now, and time and space are one, then connecting with the infinite is entirely possible, so too the feasibility of interstellar travel.

Albert Einstein propounded the existence of tunnels embedded within the fabric of the Universe; shortcuts in space/time through which a traveller could conceivably pass - the concept become known as the Wormhole Theory.

Einstein's hypothesis bears an uncanny resemblance to the tunnels reported by those who have died and live to tell their tale whilst undergoing so called Near-Death Experience.

In the mid-nineteen nineties, after reading the account of one such experience, involving the 'deceased' leaving his body and traversing the solar system before entering such a portal, I wrote to The International Association for Near-Death Studies [UK] inviting the organisation's Chairman to consider a possible link between NDE's and Einstein's conjecture. The reply I received dismissed as implausible the idea that physical and spiritual occupy the same space; it was felt the spirit realm was separate from the material realm, which to my mind entirely missed the point; it is patently apparent that spirituality and physicality are fused in human form, so why not beyond the limitations of life on earth?

From 11th December 2021 to Boxing Day 2021, the storm of mystical cognisance broke and with it the pain, tears and triumphs of past lives, clearly remembered and acutely felt in the here and now.

The meaning and importance of duality was made crystal clear. With comprehension and intense compassion I saw war, famine and pestilence. I understood that change is the only constant, that everything is interrelated, that we are all inextricably linked, that the only mistakes are those we do not learn from, and that things are ordained just so for good reason.

Synchronistic shooting stars and mysterious lights were visible in the sky, and not for the first-time dates with cosmic significance were imparted to me.

During the 90s, I received a transmission:

‘The Global Manifestation of Light in the form of Craft,
will take place on Christmas Eve 1997.’

I took this to mean that the skies of our planet would be illuminated by the Star People; the very same celestial beings that seeded us on Earth.

I planned for the advent by organising an event that was to take place on The Coach Road, also known as The Pastures, located in Straindrop, County Durham, the landing site of the radiant emerald orb I had witnessed earlier that same year.

A further communique explained that this was to be a precursor to:

'The Descent of the Light in the form of Craft.'

As Christmas 97 approached, the skies over the village were aglow; swathes of luminescent, shimmering white light danced across the horizon. The Northern Echo newspaper reported the phenomenon as a laser experiment emanating from Middlesbrough, some 29.3 miles away.

That Eve, as we gathered on the Coach Road, police turned up in an Incident Response Vehicle, demanding to know:

'Why are you here? What are you doing?'

I explained that we represented the *Intergalactic Federation* and shared the communication I'd received. The driver consulted his fellow officer:

'We should be on the streets of Darlington.'

Then sped off, leaving us to continue with preparations.

People came from far and wide to take part - Durham, Dumfries, Devon. My marvellous brothers rallied round with everyone else. Elizabeth, our amazing mother, cooked up and dished out hot broth from a cauldron to keep participants warm. Brian Russell of Little Newsham, a neighbouring hamlet, provided transport and wood fired braziers [Brian, a Master Blacksmith, went on to design and forge the entrance gates for London's Globe Theatre].

I'd arranged hundreds of flashing battery powered lights to form a circle on the ground, and on the off-chance, my suitcase was packed and ready to go!

I felt held, supported, surrounded by love and goodwill.

The proceedings were recorded by my cherished friend Chris Leger, a film maker, who I'd invited to our family home with a request that she document events.

Some weeks prior to this it was conveyed by a 'channeler', who'd arrived at my door unannounced, that although we would not observe craft on the night:

'The Star People shall be with you.'

To my knowledge there were no sightings by the those who held hands in that *Ring of Unity* we formed as Karen Carpenter's ethereal voice called out to Occupants of Interplanetary Craft; the occasion however, was not without high drama, as this all took place against a backdrop of hurricane winds that rip-roared through our ears, across the nation, into and through the night … the full force of the butterfly effect.

Flashback

Amid a recent altered state, I was overwhelmed by three lucid visions, accompanied by associated emotions, that left me troubled and grieved.

You may draw your own conclusion as to whether the following accounts are considered lunacy, hallucination, the product of an overactive imagination, or genuine past life regression.

The 1st - I'm enslaved on a cotton plantation in the deep south. A man of faith, put to work alongside a woman I adore, also of African origin.

We are released from our captivity by a humanitarian reformist who negotiates a price for our liberty. We're bestowed with enough capital to buy a modest timber house, and enabled to marry and bring in a small income. My wife gives birth to two daughters.

I'm sitting in the shade of our veranda, happy and proud, listening to the voice of my wife singing in the kitchen, our daughters are laughing and playing at my feet. I retain a secret, which gives me reason to feel victorious. The night before I'd been invited [deceitfully] to the slave owner's homestead. After dinner his daughter led me to a barn were I was seduced.

My joy and deep satisfaction is short lived, as we are confronted by an approaching lynch mob. I am separated from wife and children, who are mercilessly slaughtered in front of my eyes.

Rope tied to a tree, noose around my neck, the faces of the people below stare back at me with glee. Silently I beseech, 'Father forgive them, for they know not what they do'. The last words I hear are:

'Nigger pack your bags!'

The 2nd - The eve of the Battle of the Somme. I'm in command of a company of men from my home town. With my younger brother's approval [second in command], I announce to the troops:

'We're not going over!'

Our trench erupts with the elated cries of fellow countrymen and celebrations ensue.

An orderly is despatched to identify the cause of the din and report back to an officer.

That night, I and my brother are hauled up before the officer. I am ordered three times to rescind our decree and go into battle. Each time I respond:

'No Sir!'

My brother too is commanded to obey but also refuses.

We are condemned to face the firing squad.

In separate cells, I am served a last meal of horse steak, my brother is severally beaten. We face our executions together at dawn. The firing squad comprises a dozen comrades. Rifles at the ready, their distraught faces and tears reveal their love for us. In defiant unison, my brother and I yell our final words:

'No Sir!'

The 3rd - less detailed but no less vivid. Dorset 1938. I'm a young man standing on a lawn observing an out of control house fire raging on the top floor. Dispassionately, the knowledge that my mother is being incinerated, affirms my resolve to join the air force.

I'm flying solo over France. My plane is struck by enemy fire. I pilot the blazing craft directly into a munitions store.

Who can say if these are authentic remembered incarnations? I can say, that the intense recollections are seared into my psyche, and for me at least, remain very raw, and very real.

Star Struck

1962, aged four: I sat in a small transit van driven by Roy White, a warm hearted Caribbean painter and decorator and family friend. We were travelling through Dartmoor during the hours of darkness in the vicinity of Tavistock where my parents, having moved from London, had recently set up home. At some point during our journey my companion glanced up at the night sky and exclaimed:

'Look Aidan! Look up at the stars!'

I gazed skyward and was immediately entranced, awed by the dazzling beauty of starlight, witnessed for the very first-time.

I deluged Roy with a series of 'whys?' His patient answers awakened a wide-eyed child's imagination and triggered a lifelong quest to understand our place amongst the stars. Roy switched on the radio and was thrilled to find he'd tuned directly into the unforgettable sound of The Tornado's newly released 45rpm single 'Telstar'. It was explained that the music had a connection with our conversation and the sparkling diamonds in the sky, and I experienced yet another first, synchronicity.

During my career I have strived to exploit media and mediums that most effectively lend themselves to the conveyance of the ideas I wish to communicate; as a consequence I have utilised an eclectic mix of creative devises and disciplines - making, writing, film, photography, music, puppetry, exhibitions, performance, public speaking, public art, publishing and activism.

In 2005, responding to my encounter on the village green, I sketched onto paper an idea I called StarDisc; a 21st century stone circle.

The name emulates the oldest known accurate picture of the night sky in history, the Nebra Star Disc, a Bronze Age plate inlaid with gold about the size of a vinyl LP, discovered in Germany in 1999, which archaeologists believe to be an astronomical instrument with religious significance dated to around 1600 BC.

My objective was to create a 40ft diameter illuminated star chart carved into black granite; a Celestial Amphitheatre that would inspire and instil wonderment. In 2008, having identified the ideal site in my hometown of Wirksworth in the Derbyshire Dales, I intensified efforts to bring StarDisc into the world and set about gaining the necessary permissions, harnessing support, seeking partners and developing a fundraising campaign.

In 2011 with Arts Council England and Lottery funding, plus additional contributions from family, friends, colleagues and supporters, StarDisc was actualised. During construction my brothers and I scattered our mother's ashes into the foundations. The launch celebration was accompanied by an under the stars screening of Steven Spielberg's classic film Close Encounters of the Third Kind.

StarDisc draws on our ancient lineage, crossing cultural boundaries it combines sacred space and futuristic vision, inviting people from all walks of life to gather, contemplate and connect with whatever resides beyond the sphere of our planet.

Science is serious about the search for Extraterrestrial life. SETI [acronym: Search for Extraterrestrial Intelligence], is an organisation that was established to do precisely this. SETI was founded in 1984 with U.S. government backing. The mission of the SETI Institute is to explore, understand and explain the origin, nature and prevalence of life in the Universe. One of its many activities is to analyse radio signals that might Indicate signs of life beyond Earth. From the outset

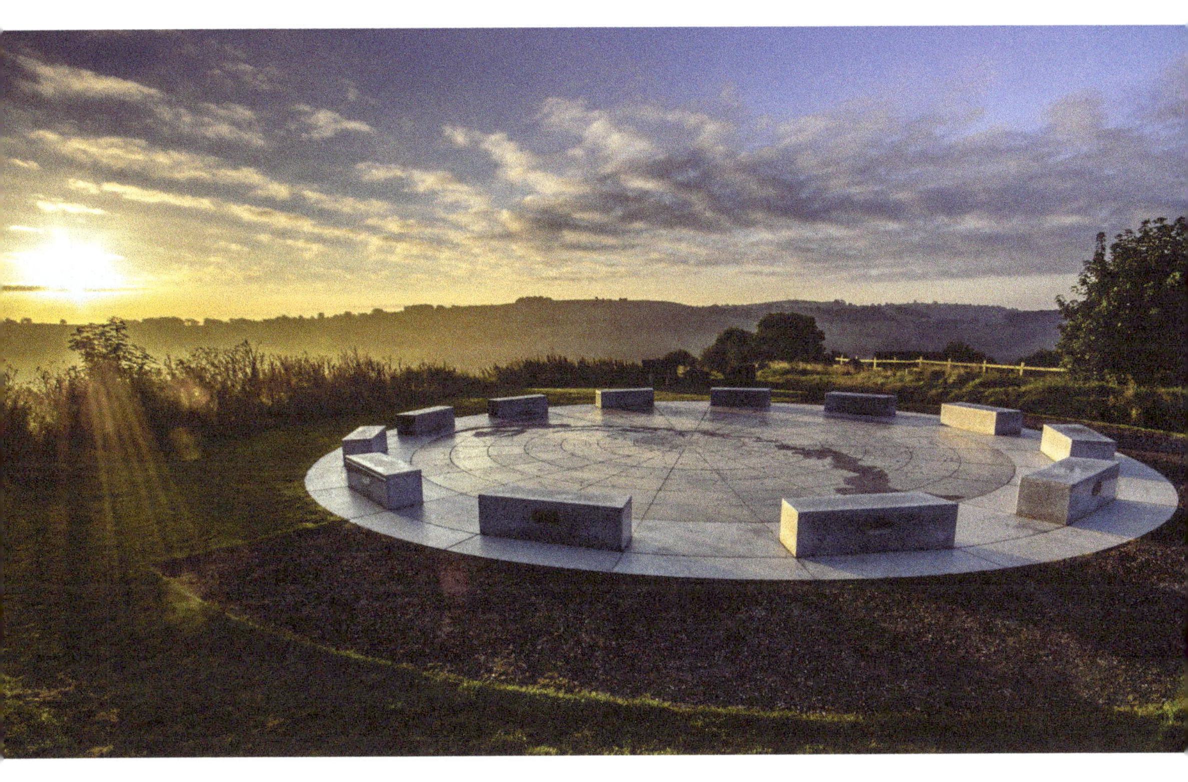

my intention was that StarDisc would share these aims; that it would facilitate transmission/reception based on the premise that each and every one of us transmits and receives as matter of course and that we need only focus our minds and project our thoughts into deep space to connect with the infinite. One can think of StarDisc as a radio telescope dish broadcasting brainwaves rather than radio waves. It has been said that thought travels faster than the speed of light - the wings on which prayers and wishes are carried.

In addition, I wanted StarDisc to be used as a platform from which to interact with UFOs and occupants, [what we now call 'UAP' - Unidentified Aerial Phenomena].

At the heart of this endeavour is a threefold ethos:
- Champion the unification of art, science and spirituality.
- Celebrate diversity, common humanity and shared cultural heritage.
- Cherish our home planet, the gift of life and our place amongst the stars.

Since its launch, I have attempted to establish new StarDiscs, and while my efforts, and those of my collaborators, have not yet yielded further commissions, we continue to innovate creative ways to manifest our shared vision - an earth-bound constellation of StarDiscs.

In a world of conflict, chaos and confusion, there is an imperative to embrace those opportunities which unite people. StarDisc offers a non-religiously or politically divisive meeting place that accepts everyone and excludes no one. *A Temple Without Walls* roofed by the sky, where religion and secularism are equally and simultaneously relevant and irrelevant, where what unites us is our individuality, diversity and shared humanity, where we can speculate about the great unknown, be open to the unexpected, and just perhaps, encounter the extraordinary.

Crystal Ball

Fearing radical change to their exclusive position in society psychiatrists cling on to their nervous system; but unless psychiatry remodels itself as an unequivocally compassionate profession and refrains from treating human beings as nothing more than bio-chemical entities, it will I assert, in the fullness of time, become redundant. I foresee psychiatry being superseded by the *Spiritual Emergence Movement* and detect evidence of this in our time.

Chemistry does not equal Anima, Anima equals Soul. *Psyche* means soul, love, life. So to care for the soul with love, one must first accept the reality of the soul and the importance of love in life.

I envisage spiritually orientated environments being established; shelters that provide true sanctuary and protect individuals experiencing unusual states. Places people are drawn to for refuge and restoration, rather than disturbed and disturbing institutions that control, manipulate, and impose pseudo-scientific doctrines and methods upon those they claim to help, in the name of authority, under the guise of care. I predict these non-threatening sanctuaries flourishing as their value comes to be recognised.

The promise of a beckoning new age invites us all to re-evaluate, re-affirm and re-awaken our humanity, with awareness of, and restored emphasis on, our intrinsic spirituality. The young shoots of this spiritual emergence are already visible; permeating all walks of life and arising in areas as diverse as the green movement, quantum physics, cosmology, parapsychology, holistic healing, the arts, popular culture, contemporary esotericism, even commercial advertising ... the future is bright. As this approaching epoch is ushered in there will be much to shed. If psychiatry does not rid itself of its inhumanity, humanity will I trust, rid itself of psychiatry.

Prophesy

Everything is going to be all right.

Angel

Postscript

In 2020 after two decades of stability I felt it was worth testing the waters to determine if my balance could be maintained without major tranquilisers.

Over a period of five months, with the use of a nail file, I gradually reduced the dosage to zero.

During the weeks that followed my spirits were buoyant. I was proud of what felt like a monumental achievement. Everything appeared to have gone well amidst a backdrop of a changed world which seemed to have gone stark raving mad at precisely the same time I'd reclaimed sanity. My soundness of mind was in sharp contrast to the hysteria spawned by the outbreak of the Corona Virus Pandemic.

I spent my days tending StarDisc in spring sunshine, where I'd sweep the Milky Way, paint the stars, pick up litter, mow grass and converse with visitors. I listened to so many absurdities while on site - 'G-5 Covid 19 cover-up', 'Revenge of the Lizards', 'Permanent Police State', 'Governments Eugenics Programme', conspiracy theories everywhere! My response was, everyone get a grip and get off my cloud, I'm the Paranoid Schizo!

Then, quite suddenly, on receiving the transmission 'Everything is as it should be', I lost my own grip on reality, was seen by a mental health crisis team, and admitted to hospital.

Twenty two years prior to this I'd been treated deplorably in the same Psychiatric Unit. Although I, and fellow activists had campaigned for many years I was unaware our calls to end Psychiatric Assault had been taken seriously, I anticipated the worst.

But in the summer of that year, during a nine week section, against all expectations, it transpired our cries had been heard and heeded.

Much had improved. I and my companions on the ward were treated with dignity and respect; I felt consultants and nursing staff genuinely had our welfare at heart.

That said, my jaw hit the floor when it was deemed that my life time diagnosis should be dismissed in favour of 'Bipolar Disorder', only to be reinstated when I explained that I was not afflicted by depression! The irony of receiving a contradictory second opinion after forty two years was priceless.

Whilst my unease about institutional settings prevails, and of course there were faults [further improvements are most definitely required], there is reason to be hopeful. At last in our country, after centuries of maltreatment, attitudes seem to be changing, and a belated overhaul of the mental health system occurring.

As for me, knowing positive reforms are being implemented brings its own kind of healing, and though I continue to take the tablets, or to be precise monthly depot injections [administered in the arm!], I remain deeply grateful for the miracle of life, and can say that in my world, truly, everything is alright.

Acknowledgements

Kindred spirits at John Connolly Psychiatric Unit, Birmingham -1978.
The Piermont Psychiatric Unit, Darlington Memorial Hospital -1998.
Phase 3 Psychiatric Unit, Derby City General Hospital -1998.
Radbourne Psychiatric Unit, Royal Derby Hospital - 2020.
The Spinney, Hulton PICU Ward, Greater Manchester - 2022. * * * * *

Fellow mental health reform campaigners, for keeping the faith.

Sir Norman Lamb, Minister of State for Care and Support 2012-2015, for acknowledging the negative impact of Psychiatric Assault and initiating the Positive and Proactive Care Policy ... Thank you!

Roy White, for opening my eyes to wonders of the Universe.

Friends and colleagues for their support and encouragement.

Departed loved ones Chris Ledger and Deborah Rose - missing you.

Collaborators Anna Clyne, Steve Wood, Louise Trevett, Phil Bramall, Mike Gulliford, Jude Irons, Morgan Barke, for keeping the dream alive.

Best Man Langley Brown, for his loyalty and solidarity.

Donald and Elizabeth, my father and mother, for shielding me from the psychiatric system, facilitating my creative development and instilling confidence.

Brothers Crispin, Dickon, Luke, and sisters in - law Christine, Naomi, for sharing the tears and laughter, pain and joy.

Step-son and companion Pierce, for being a star.

My wife Tricia, for her understanding, wise counsel and deep compassion [now living independently].

Photographers

Roger Lee: 33 / 49

Jan Schouten: 91

Ben Johnson: 113 / 114

Jim Bell: 153

Anthony Fisher: 137 / 162

Aidan Shingler: Additional photography and original artwork.

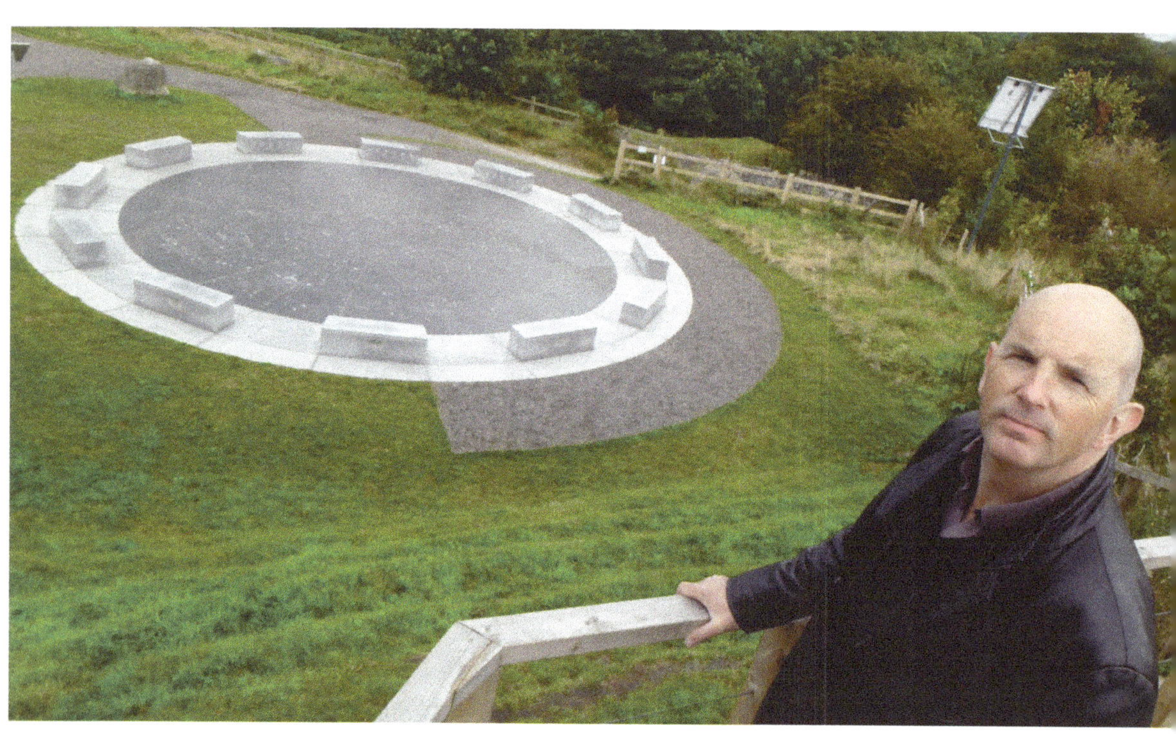

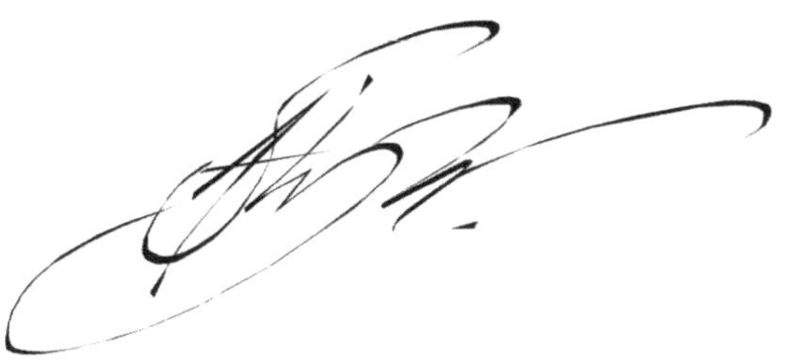

9 781953 882196